Thou

.

Archbishop Marcel Lefebvre

# THOUGHT
# FOR THE DAY

Texts selected by the Sisters of
the Society of Saint Pius X

Translated by Michael J. Miller

Angelus
Press

PO Box 217
St. Marys, KS 66536

Original edition: *Une pensée par jour*, Collection Itinéraire
Spirituel, Clovis, 2019

**Library of Congress Cataloging-in-Publication Data**
Names: Lefebvre, Marcel, 1905-1991, author. | Miller, Michael J.,
    translator.
Title: A thought for the day : texts selected by the Sisters of the Society
    of Saint Pius X / translated by Michael J. Miller.
Other titles: Pensée par jour. English
Description: Saint Marys, KS : Angelus Press, [2021] | "Original edition:
    Une pensée par jour, Collection Itinéraire Spirituel, Clovis, 2019." |
    Summary: "A thought for each day of the year from Archbishop Marcel
    Lefebvre"-- Provided by publisher.
Identifiers: LCCN 2021021985 | ISBN 9781949124873
Subjects: LCSH: Devotional calendars--Catholic Church.
Classification: LCC BX2170.C56 L4413 2021 | DDC 242/.2--dc23
LC record available at https://lccn.loc.gov/2021021985

**ANGELUS PRESS**
PO Box 217
Saint Marys, Kansas 66536
Phone (816) 753-3150
Fax (816) 753-3557
Order Line 1-800-966-7337
**www.angeluspress.org**

ISBN: 978-1-949124-87-3
First Printing–June 2021

Printed in the United States of America

# JANUARY

The shepherds, the magi, the Holy
Family, and our life in God

---

## 1                  Circumcision of Our Lord

Today, the Feast of the Circumcision of Our
Lord reminds us about the Sacrament of Baptism.
In this sacrament we received the very same gifts
that Our Lord Jesus Christ came to bring to us
here on earth. We should reflect today particularly
on the greatness of our Baptism, and we should
harbor a ceaseless desire to grow in the knowledge
of Our Lord Jesus Christ, in our love for Him, in
this union with Our Lord Jesus Christ.

---

## 2                  Holy Name of Jesus

"His name is like oil poured out" (Saint Bernard). And this saint explains: "Oil illumines, oil
heals, oil nourishes; the Name of Jesus, too, since

Jesus illumines us, Jesus heals us, Jesus nourishes us." How beautiful it is, this comparison of the Holy Name of Jesus to oil, and how true it is! Our souls are blinded by sin; our souls are entirely preoccupied with earthly realities and forget the heavenly realities: Our Lord Jesus Christ came to remind us that we were made for Heaven, for the heavenly realities that are eternal.

---

# 3 Saint Genevieve
*Virgin*

What will this New Year be for us? God only knows, but by our desire for sanctification we can turn for help to Our Lord's will to save our soul and all souls. How consoling it is to think that our everyday life can be transformed into numerous graces of sanctification and Redemption! So it was throughout the life of Our Lord and of the Virgin Mary.

---

# 4 Saint Angela of Foligno
*Widow*

When the shepherds went into the cave, they found the Infant Jesus, and having come to this

Infant, they were filled with heavenly gifts. They understood that He was God. We, in contrast, run the risk of marveling at this little Infant Jesus, born of the Virgin Mary, yet not being in the same atmosphere as the shepherds who had just heard the angels singing His praises. We must give this Infant the divine dimensions that are rightly His.

## 5 Saint Telesphorus
*Pope and Martyr*

The star was a ray from heaven that illumined the intellects and the minds of the magi and made them fall prostrate before this Child. They understood that this was truly the Son of God. Let us not limit the Person of the Word to this body, nor even to this soul that animates this body. God is still God. God is the one who speaks through this soul and this body, and at the same time sustains the entire world.

## 6 Epiphany of Our Lord

Several earthly kings came to adore Our Lord Jesus Christ. They recognized in Him the One who was truly their King. And how is His royalty manifested in a particular way in us and in the world? Why did Our Lord Jesus Christ come to reign on earth as He does in heaven? So that we might carry out His holy will. His will is that the law of love might reign, the law of charity that He inscribed in the hearts of all human beings at the moment of their birth.

---

## 7                     Saint Clerus

*Deacon*

"Tell us, what have you seen? Tell us!" Indeed, is there anything more important and more urgent for us than to know what they went to see, what they saw, why they went to that Child in Bethlehem? Here is what the shepherds answered: "The King of Heaven deigned to be born of the Virgin Mary so as to lead lost man back to Heaven...." That is the summary of what the shepherds were able to learn from the angels, from the Blessed Virgin, and from Saint Joseph. This Child is the King of Heaven, the One whom Heaven and earth cannot contain: He is hidden in that Child's flesh.

# 8      Saint Lucian of Beauvais

*Martyr*

Our Lord wanted the shepherds to come and adore Him within a family. Indeed, in a way the shepherds came to honor the family itself, not only the Child, but also Mary and Joseph.

---

# 9      Saint Julian of Antioch

*Martyr*

The magi came to adore the Child and they offered Him their gifts, which symbolize His essential, fundamental attributes: gold—the King; incense—the priesthood and the Priest; myrrh—the Savior. These are the three major attributes of Our Lord Jesus Christ, but in adoring the Child, the splendor of that adoration was reflected also on Mary and on Joseph, on the family.

---

# 10      Saint Agatho

*Pope*

Jesus willed to live in that family for thirty years out of the thirty-three that He lived here on earth. What can be the meaning of such an extended stay? It is not that He needed it, since He was the one who gave to the home of Mary and Joseph all its good qualities. But He wanted to remain in that family precisely to show the importance of the family, the family that prepares the children who emerge from it for their mission, as Jesus wanted to prepare Himself for His mission within that family. What a great lesson!

# 11 Saint Hyginus
*Pope and Martyr*

The Word of God became incarnate only once, but His Incarnation is prolonged. From now on it exists in eternity. Certainly, Jesus Christ is in Heaven with His risen body and now He is glorious for all eternity, but He wishes to come among us under the appearances of bread and wine so that we might adore Him, as the shepherds adored Him in the crib, as the Virgin Mary and Saint Joseph adored Him.

## 12 — Saint Tatiana
*Martyr*

Let us ask Saint Joseph to enlighten us about this mystery, since he lived for thirty years in intimate union with the great mystery, for the great mystery of our holy religion is Our Lord Jesus Christ, God incarnate humbling Himself to the point of taking a body like ours and a soul like ours and parents like the ones we have. Saint Joseph was in the same house, he lived with Our Lord, he worked with his hands together with Him, he spoke with Him as a close relative for thirty years.

## 13 — Baptism of Our Lord

Let us make a resolution, at the start of this year, to live with the Good Lord, under His watchful eye, to love Him with all our heart, to love Our Lord Jesus Christ. He is within us. We live with Him especially when we receive Him in Holy Communion. And may we keep Him within us not only in Holy Communion, but every day and all day long.

# 14        Saint Hilary of Poitiers

*Bishop and Doctor*

See the humility of the Most Blessed Virgin, her self-effacing simplicity. See the modesty of Saint Joseph. Not one word spoken by Saint Joseph has been recorded. And yet, he is certainly the greatest saint after the Most Blessed Virgin! He must have had unequaled sanctity and virtues, since God chose him to be the guardian, the one in charge, and even the head of the family of God Himself.

---

# 15        Saint Paul

*Hermit and Confessor*

Our Lord wanted things to be done in an ordinary way; He wanted to live like us, as much like us as possible, and to allow the Most Blessed Virgin and Saint Joseph to suffer because of Him. He could have spared them these sufferings—that is obvious and clear. But no, Our Lord wanted them to have those trials. In accepting them with their whole heart, they had the merit of suffering for Our Lord.

# 16 Saint Marcellus I
*Pope and Martyr*

When the Virgin Mary and Saint Joseph looked for shelter at an inn, they were sent away; someone told them that there was no room for them. Isn't this just like what Our Lord Jesus Christ has gone though over the centuries in His humanity and in His Church? No one accepts Our Lord Jesus Christ. There are many who are against Him, those who have denied everything that He did and still does today to redeem us, to apply His blood to us, to apply His redemption to us.

# 17 Saint Anthony
*Abbot*

Henceforth all souls, as soon as they are born, ought to turn to Our Lord Jesus Christ to receive supernatural life: natural life is nothing unless there is supernatural life. God willed that this life of grace, this divine life, the life of the Holy Trinity should exist in us. This is the reason why He came! And consequently unless our nature bears this wonderful fruit, flourishes with this extraordinary unfolding of supernatural life, it is of no use. It is like a candlestick that has no candle and no flame.

---

## 18           Saint Prisca
*Virgin and Martyr*

If we really want Our Lord Jesus Christ to be our king, let us try to imagine what Nazareth must have been like: Jesus, Mary, and Joseph. What must Mary have thought of Jesus? What must Joseph have thought of Jesus? This is a great mystery, an unfathomable mystery of God's goodness and charity, to think that He chose two creatures and allowed them to live with Him in close proximity to Jesus, to the One who is God, without whom neither Mary nor Joseph could speak or think or live.

---

## 19    Saint Marius and Companions
*Martyrs*

Saint Joseph was the head, the foster father, and the guardian of the Holy Family. For thirty years out of thirty-three, God was subject to His adoptive father. Saint Joseph gave orders to the

One who made the world, heaven and earth, everything, who set the stars in the firmament, who created the Blessed Virgin Mary. And yet Saint Joseph was a model of humility. He remained silent and humble in adoring Our Lord Jesus Christ. His only love was for Jesus.

## 20     Saints Fabian and Sebastian
*Martyrs*

In order to persevere in the faith, in order to preserve the honor of our only Lord and king, Jesus Christ, the Son of God, God eternal, we cannot be preoccupied with our feelings; now we have only one: the sense of loyalty and fidelity, whatever happens, whatever may come.

## 21     Saint Agnes
*Virgin and Martyr*

How can we help gazing on the Infant Jesus, on Mary and Joseph? May the sentiments and the thoughts that make our hearts beat more quickly be ours today and every day of the year.

# 22 Saints Vincent and Anastasius
*Martyrs*

Our hearts join with those of Mary and Joseph and the shepherds to sing with the angels our hymn of thanksgiving, because a Savior is given to us, the heavens are open; the Way, the Truth, and the Life are given to us so that we can arrive there.

---

# 23 Saint Raymond of Penyafort
*Confessor*

By mysterious means which He Himself chose, Our Lord Jesus Christ now draws souls to Himself, to bring them into the intimacy of this family of God. He willed to come and dwell among us, wanted us to be temples of the Holy Ghost already here on earth. Our Lord never stops calling these souls to a greater union with Him, to a greater union with the Most Holy Trinity.

---

# 24 Saint Timothy
*Bishop and Martyr*

Our Lord is here among us. He is here with the same flesh that He had when He was in the crib, the flesh that He took from the virginal flesh of Mary. In all the hymns that we have sung tonight, the Virgin Mary was intimately associated with the glory of Our Lord Jesus Christ. Similarly, the Most Blessed Virgin Mary too is a sign of contradiction: you are either for her or against her. Some would like to do away with this great privilege of her divine motherhood, her perpetual virginity. Some would like to tarnish the virginity of Mary.

---

# 25      Conversion of Saint Paul
*Apostle*

Our living faith will produce real fruits of charity if we understand that our life must first be contemplative, I would like to say mystical, in the true sense of the word, captivated by the mystery of God, of Our Lord Jesus Christ.

---

# 26      Saint Polycarp
*Bishop and Martyr*

We must be present to the Most Blessed Virgin in all her life and imitate her. In our lives we will all have trials, some of us more, some fewer;

let us ask her to help us to bear them as she herself did courageously.

## 27       Saint John Chrysostom

*Bishop, Doctor*

We must remember often this saying of Saint Paul and meditate on it: "*Non est longe*—He is not far," He is here! "In Him we live and move and are" [Acts 17:27-28], so that we can say: "My God, You are here, I love You. My God, I want only You. I want to live only for You. You are my all."

## 28       Saint Peter Nolasco

*Confessor*

Let us live constantly with Our Lord, in all our difficulties, our trials, our desires, so that everything is subject to Him. Let us never be caught napping and alone, when we can have the help of the One who created us, who died for us on the cross, and who comes into our hearts.

# 29        Saint Francis de Sales
*Bishop and Doctor*

Our apostolate will be strictly supernatural in all its motives if it is intended for the glory and the kingdom of Our Lord, exclusively. Visible or hidden success will matter little to us. The number of souls, great or small, will not preoccupy us. "A single soul is a large diocese," Saint Francis de Sales used to say. This will be the secret of our tireless zeal, which is never discouraged by trials or lack of success, by obstacles or opposition, even by our brethren.

---

# 30        Saint Martha
*Virgin and Martyr*

Thirty out of thirty-three years in simple, humble work, with Saint Joseph, in family life, show us that this is the life that we should live, a simple, humble life which at the same time is entirely devoted to prayer.

# 31 Saint John Bosco

*Confessor*

You will have to help parents to sanctify their children, and you already do this as much as you can. In doing so, you will remember to have faith in the supernatural means for the sanctification of souls because, in many priests, this faith has diminished, and to a certain extent they have even lost their faith in the efficacy of the good Lord's grace.

# FEBRUARY

Prayer, adoration, the Divine Office

---

## 1      Saint Ignatius of Antioch
*Bishop and Martyr*

God is entirely present everywhere, and consequently in us. We do not have to make great efforts to find God. He is here, He is with us! Whether we are coming or going, wherever we may be, God is always with us.

---

## 2   Presentation of Jesus in the Temple

Present yourself like Jesus in the Temple, with a pure, detached heart, and ask Mary to present you in the Temple, like Our Lord. You are her children. Ask her to place in your souls, in your hearts, the dispositions that she had when she herself presented her divine Son there.

# 3 Saint Blaise
*Bishop and Martyr*

There are several ways to pray: vocal prayer, which we do for example at Mass; mental prayer, like the prayer of those who come to recollect themselves for a while before the Blessed Sacrament or who read a book on spirituality for some time in order to have good thoughts, to set their mind in the right attitude toward the good Lord and to be united with Him.

---

# 4 Saint Andrew Corsini
*Bishop*

Yet there is a kind of prayer which, I would say, is even more essential, and this is the kind which the good Lord asks us to be engaged in always: the prayer of the heart. This prayer of the heart is our love for the good Lord, and this love must never cease. Just as children think frequently, almost continually of their parents, so too we should have our heart directed toward the good Lord, throughout our life. This is true prayer, deep prayer, constant adoration, thanksgiving for all the benefits that the good Lord has given to us, and regret for our sins.

---

## 5            Saint Agatha
*Virgin and Martyr*

In Heaven the elevation of our souls will remain, enabling us to see the glory of the Holy Trinity. But even here below, God gives us this grace, which raises us by His Holy Spirit. Consequently we have, even here below, this union with God, with the Holy Trinity, through faith, hope, and charity.

---

## 6            Saint Titus
*Bishop and Confessor*

The life of prayer is the first manifestation of charity: love and adoration of the Father who is in Heaven through His divine Son and His Spirit.

When we adore Our Lord, we adore God, the Holy Trinity. Everything is there for us. Heaven will be nothing else.

# 7         Saint Romuald
*Abbot*

If we truly loved God with all our heart, if we adored Him as perfectly as possible, we would love our neighbor also and we would obey all the laws of charity.

---

# 8         Saint John of Matha
*Confessor*

To pray is to give one's soul to the good Lord. Consequently it is to offer Him all that we are, all that we have. It is to offer Him our intellect to receive the truth. It is to offer Him our will to carry out His.

---

# 9         Saint Cyril of Alexandria
*Bishop, Confessor, and Doctor*

If you feel that you are having too much trouble concentrating to pray, take a book of prayers, recite the Our Father, for example, or the Creed slowly, very gently, phrase after phrase, while reflecting and trying to concentrate your mind on these prayers.

# 10 Saint Scholastica
*Virgin*

As God, Our Lord knows everything, and since His knowledge is communicated to His soul, even as man Our Lord knows things through the communication that He has from the Word. He knows us better than our parents do. This is why our prayer must be union with a Person who knows us perfectly, who knows all that we are.

# 11 The Apparition of Our Lady of Lourdes

Prayer is love. In this way a child is happy at his mother's side. He remains there, near her, and says nothing. We ought to be like that too with the good Lord. If someone separated us from Him, we should not tolerate it. Now, we can be everywhere with God, everywhere.

# 12 The Seven Holy Founders of the Servites

What is the posture that conveys adoration? Well, it is kneeling down! "Man is never as great as when he is on his knees." Why? Because a man who adores grows taller! Someone who adores God, someone who puts himself in the true posture that he should have before God, makes himself greater in God's eyes.

---

## 13            Saint Polyeuctus
*Martyr*

"I am come to cast fire on the earth. And what will I, but that it be kindled?" (Lk. 12:49). This fire is the Holy Ghost, the Spirit of charity who fills the Holy Trinity and who created spirits in order to inflame them with this charity. This conflagration is the prayer of every soul adoring her Creator and Redeemer, and entrusting herself to His holy will in imitation of Jesus crucified, offering His life in a surge of charity toward His Father and to save souls.

---

## 14            Saint Valentine
*Priest and Martyr*

I would almost say that we have to be with the good Lord even if we have no words to say to Him, even if we have no external things to express to Him. The mere fact of being at God's side, at Our Lord's side, is enough; the mere fact that we are there, that we have the intention to give ourselves completely to the good Lord, to entrust ourselves to him. This is true prayer, interior prayer, the prayer that sanctifies us.

## 15      Saint Faustinus and Jovita
*Martyrs*

By praising God, by setting before our eyes His greatness, His omnipotence, His goodness, and His mercy, little by little we put ourselves too in the place that belongs to us, namely humility, that is to say, the truth. If we truly esteem God for what He is, our humility increases more and more, then our soul is engulfed in adoration of God, of that Being who surpasses us so much, who is so far above us.

## 16      Saint Juliana of Nicomedia
*Virgin*

The older I get, the more I think that prayer of the heart is what transforms the soul and puts it in a state of continual offering. This is what vocal and mental prayers should lead to. If contemplation is a look of love at Jesus crucified and glorified, then it transports the soul into God's hands so as to carry out His holy will.

---

# 17 Saint Julian of Cappadocia
### *Martyr*

Many people have the impression that when they went to Mass on Sunday or performed some religious act during the week, afterwards that was it. But prayer should be a continual interior attitude. No doubt, we cannot pray all the time, we have our occupations. But we must keep this interior disposition, in other words, this spirit of adoring God interiorly which makes a person entirely subject to him, totally in His hands, always desiring to do His will.

---

# 18 Saint Simeon of Jerusalem
### *Bishop and Martyr*

All the saints led the life of prayer, which is simultaneously an effect and a cause of holiness. This was because they had a very extensive idea of this life of prayer which reaches even the will and the heart, and thus achieves the purpose for which God created and redeemed us—adoring God in a total offering of ourselves, after the example of Our Lord, who came into this world and said to His Father: "*Ecce venio ut faciam voluntatem tuam.*" "Behold, I come to do Thy will." (Hebrews 10:9)

---

# 19             Saint Gavin
*Bishop and Martyr*

While saying prayers, like the Rosary that we sometimes recite a bit monotonously, we can very well have our mind turned completely to God. A person who prays that way is thinking of nothing but Our Lord, of God, of the holy angels, of Heaven. His prayer is probably more pleasing to God than the prayer of someone who tries to pay attention to all the words that he pronounces. The important thing is to have one's mind turned toward God, toward Our Lord, who is the object of the prayer.

# 20     Saint Eucherius of Orleans
*Bishop*

Meditating on the soul of Our Lord should give us the immense desire for Him to take possession of our soul more and more, so that we can be, in a certain way, extensions of Him. This is what God intended in creating us: that we truly be souls and bodies that Our Lord can occupy, that He can take charge of in order to sing the praises and glory of God His Father and fill them with His Spirit.

---

# 21     Blessed Noël Pinot
*Martyr*

I think that during this era in which we live, this era of the Church which is so troubled, more than ever the Church needs your prayers. Therefore I take the liberty of insisting on your spirit of prayer, your union with Our Lord, so as to beg the Almighty, to beg Our Lord to come to the help of His Church, to come to the help of the priesthood in particular, with your eyes fixed on the cross of Our Lord Jesus Christ.

# 22 Chair of Saint Peter (in Antioch)
*Apostle*

Prayer must be above all interior, as it will be in Heaven. This elevation of our souls to God causes our souls to become detached from themselves, from every temporal preoccupation, so as to belong entirely to God.

As we deepen both the nature of our prayer and the extension of it into our human and Christian life, we will be convinced that the deep life of the created and redeemed soul must be a life of continual prayer.

---

# 23 Saint Peter Damian
*Bishop, Confessor, and Doctor*

Development of the spirit of prayer corresponds to the development of the spiritual life. As long as you are not purified, when you seek to enter into prayer, imagination and memory start to work and the spirit is gone.... Then you must return to God slowly, peacefully. You must not lose patience and be annoyed at yourself, saying: "I can't manage to pray, to concentrate; I am always distracted." You won't succeed by becoming irritated with yourself. You must ask Our Lord for the grace of prayer and gently silence all that may disturb it.

---

## 24                 Saint Matthias

*Apostle*

Our Lord founded His Church to honor Him, to sing His glory, to sing His praises, to imitate Him, to share in His divine life. That is what the Church is.

The liturgy is the public prayer of the Church. This prayer was entrusted to the Apostles by Our Lord and is handed on to us by the Church. This is why we thank the Church for having given us this whole beautiful liturgy which she places on the lips of Christians throughout the world.

---

## 25             Saint Cesarius of Nazianz

*Confessor*

The liturgy is a school of humility. You see it by the gestures, by the bows, the genuflections, the great respect that people have for God in the liturgy, by the incensations, the profound bows, and the respect that the participants have for each other.

---

# 26     Saint Victor of Arcis-sur-Aube
*Bishop*

You see that the liturgy always has us pray through Our Lord Jesus Christ, with Him, in Him. The Church refrains from giving us a religion in which Our Lord would not intervene. For her, Our Lord is everything; she is His mystical Bride. She makes sure not to forget it. This is why our prayers conclude each time with the words: *per Christum Dominum nostrum*—through Christ Our Lord. By this we see that no one can obtain any grace apart from Him.

---

# 27     Saint Gabriel of the Sorrowful Mother
*Confessor*

The Church begets souls, nourishes them, and transforms them in and through her liturgy. We can say in truth that the liturgy really is the Church's womb where souls find all their nourishment, the perfect food of their spiritual life, an appreciation for the true values and the hierarchy among them, and an apprenticeship in all the virtues.

---

## 28      Saint Romanus of Lyons
*Abbot*

"*Gloria Patri, et Filio, et Spiritui Sancto in saecula saeculorum. Amen.*" "Glory be to the Father, and to the Son, and to the Holy Ghost, now and forever. Amen." This is the most beautiful prayer that you pray; don't forget that! This is the conclusion of the recitation of the psalms. The Church decided to put this prayer at the end of the psalms because it is, so to speak, the conclusion, the splendid effect of every prayer. We cannot pray any better than to say: "*Gloria Patri... Amen.*" This is the most beautiful prayer that we can pray.

# 29           Saint Dositheus

*Confessor*

Contemplation is part of Christian life; it is the life of faith, the life of the spirit of faith. Contemplation consists of dwelling on all the realities of our faith.

Prayer is truly the act that unites us to the good Lord here below, that removes us from all the cares of this earth, of this world, and unites us to God so that we may always carry out His holy will.

# MARCH

## Redemption

---

### 1   Saint Albinus of Angers
*Bishop*

Our faith, our sanctification, and our salvation are accomplished through the cross of Our Lord. Everything is accomplished through Christ's death on the cross. For us this must be a subject of continual meditation.

---

### 2   Saint Agnes of Prague
*Virgin*

Our Lord is not only our model, but also the cause of our resurrection, of our sanctification; in Him we truly find all that we need for our sanctification.

# 3        Saint Martin
*Soldier and Martyr*

God manifests His mercy, this is certain; we observe it, and Our Lord's whole life manifests it, His passion and death in particular. "*Mater misericordiae*, Mother of mercy," is a title that draws down special graces for us, both from Our Lord and from the Most Blessed Virgin Mary.

---

# 4        Saint Casimir
*Confessor*

We must be souls that desire and seek God. We must fight against sin, no doubt, but not only that, and one way of fighting against it is precisely to desire God. The more ardent the soul is, the more it is consumed, in a way, by the desire to be united to God, to love Him, the more it will distance itself from sin, and in the same measure.

---

# 5        Saint John Joseph of the Cross
*Confessor*

The spiritual life is a form of combat. We must fight. Let us fight courageously, with the conviction that one day Our Lord will give us the victory, but let us use the means of winning it. Let us use the means, which are the pursuit of sanctity and above all the cross of Our Lord, which is the path to the resurrection. Our resurrection comes about by way of the altar, Holy Mass, the sacrifice of the cross.

---

# 6    Saints Felicity and Perpetua
*Martyrs*

Our Lord, who is the rich man par excellence—the innately rich man, since He has heaven and earth at His disposal—conquered concupiscence by His poverty. He was poor in every way, until His death. Through the cross, Our Lord conquered the spirit of the world that makes us forget the goods of Heaven by attaching us inordinately to earthly goods.

---

# 7    Saint Thomas Aquinas
*Confessor and Doctor*

If we believe that Our Lord Jesus Christ is God and that He is the one nailed to the wood of the cross, this has immediate consequences for our life in practice, our everyday life, at every moment. This changes our life.

---

# 8                 Saint John of God
### *Confessor*

We do not understand correctly the reason why Our Lord came unless we enter into the atmosphere of the mercy of Our Lord Jesus, the Savior, and consequently into the context of sinful human beings.

---

# 9            Saint Frances of Rome
### *Widow*

People are astounded and do not dare to think it possible that God, in His infinite mercy, in His omnipotence, in His greatness, having the sin of man before His eyes, should have had the idea to come and offer Himself and to suffer on the cross to save him, to redeem him, and thus to show him His mercy in an absolutely extraordinary way.

# 10         Forty Martyrs of Sebaste

What attitude will human beings take? Some do not hesitate to present themselves to the physician of their souls and to ask forgiveness for their sins and to ask Our Lord to apply the graces and gifts of His mercy so as to be saved.

---

# 11         Saint Firmin
*Abbot*

We must have this desire to imitate Our Lord, to be victims on the cross like Him. It is necessary to ask Our Lord and the Blessed Virgin for this grace of detachment.

---

# 12         Saint Gregory the Great
*Pope, Confessor, and Doctor*

To have faith without holiness is to have theory without practice. It is very good to have faith, but if you do not put it into practice through holiness, it is worthless.

# 13       Saint Patricia
*Virgin and Martyr*

She, the Virgin Mary, had faith. Behind those wounds, behind His pierced heart, she saw God, her divine Son. We too, despite the wounds of the Church, despite the difficulties that we are undergoing, despite persecution, do not abandon Holy Mother Church!

---

# 14       Saint Mathilda
*Queen and Widow*

Our Lord Jesus Christ is truly the way by which we must acquire holiness; we must be sanctified through Jesus, in Jesus, with Jesus, consequently by meditating on Our Lord's perfections and His words.

---

# 15       Saint Louise de Marillac
*Widow*

The cross is what will make us win our victory. The cross, in other words, sacrifice. We must not be afraid of this word: sacrifice. We must sacrifice ourselves, die to all our bad inclinations, to all our bad instincts, to the sins that are in us. We must act in such a way that they die through the cross of Our Lord.

---

# 16       Saint John Brebeuf
*Martyr*

May our crucifix truly be for us the book of our meditations, because everything is summed up in Our Lord's cross: His divinity, therefore the mystery of the Incarnation, the mystery of Redemption, the mystery of the Holy Trinity.

---

# 17       Saint Patrick
*Bishop and Confessor*

The sight of the cross and the sight of the living cross, which is Holy Mass, help us greatly. Indeed, through the cross, Our Lord was victorious over sin, death, and the devil. The cross therefore symbolizes Our Lord's victory. For us, it is an encouragement: it is necessary for us to be victorious too through the cross!

# 18       Saint Cyril of Jerusalem

*Bishop, Confessor, and Doctor*

Mercy is the source of sacrifice. It impels a person to sacrifice, because it is the readiness to give oneself totally, so that charity may be restored in hearts.

---

# 19       Saint Joseph, Spouse of the Blessed Virgin Mary

After the Blessed Virgin, no one had as many graces concerning Our Lord than Saint Joseph. God chose him to be the guardian and the spouse of the Virgin Mary. We should pray to him often to ask him for lights.

---

# 20       Saint Archippus

*Confessor*

We make progress in the virtue of humility by meditating on the passion of Christ. Why? Because Our Lord, in His humiliation, gives us precisely an example of humility.

# 21        Saint Benedict
*Abbot*

The tree in paradise which was the cause of man's fall is now countered by the tree of the cross which was the cause of our redemption, and the fruit of this tree of the cross is Our Lord, with whom we commune every day.

---

# 22        Saint Leah
*Widow*

The cross is the deepest, the most admirable expression of what Our Lord Jesus Christ, true God and true man, did for us.

---

# 23        Saint Joseph Oriol
*Confessor*

All graces come from the cross, from Calvary, from the pierced heart from which flowed blood and water. The blood represents the Sacrifice of the Mass, and the water represents the Baptism which washes away sins.

# 24        Saint Gabriel
### *Archangel*

Let us take our place and stand beside the Most Blessed Virgin and Our Lord on Calvary, and let us ask the Most Blessed Virgin to help us to have faith, to believe that this man, who is nailed to the cross in such a pitiful state, is God.

---

# 25       Annunciation to the Blessed Virgin Mary

God Himself is the one who chose the Virgin Mary to be His Mother, and by that very fact our Mother, because she is the Mother of Jesus and therefore of all the members of the Mystical Body of Jesus. A child who rejects his mother is a turncoat. Devotion to the Blessed Virgin is therefore not an optional devotion.

---

# 26       Saint Emmanuel
### *Martyr*

It is enough to contemplate Our Lord nailed to the cross, covered with blood, crowned with thorns, His side open, to see that He has truly conquered the world. From now on, by the royal road of the cross, Heaven is open, and souls can follow Our Lord and go up into it. Sin has been conquered.

# 27     Saint John Damascene
*Doctor*

Our Lord Jesus Christ did not die by the thrust of the lance that He received in His heart. He died of love. Our Lord's soul escaped from His body because He willed it. He died of love for His Father, first of all, and then out of love for us, so as to restore the bond between humanity and His Father.

# 28     Saint John of Capistrano
*Confessor*

What did Our Lord Jesus Christ do on the cross to strengthen us in faith? He gave us an extraordinary gift to strengthen us in the faith, to keep us on the path to Heaven and to confirm us in grace. Our Lord found no other way but to give us His Mother!

# 29  48 Blessed Martyrs of Toulouse

It is truly instructive, enlightening, to see how much Our Lord fulfilled all the Beatitudes on the cross. If we want to share in the Beatitudes, which are the crowning of the Holy Ghost in souls, we must also share in Our Lord's life, in His cross.

---

# 30  Saint Rieul of Arles
*Bishop*

Our Lord's sacrifice is at the heart of human history, in order to sanctify all humanity and bring it to God, to make all human beings sing the praises of God and His glory.

---

# 31  Saint Benjamin
*Deacon and Martyr*

Baptism, through which we die to our sins and rise again to divine life, is signified by the death of Jesus on the cross and by His Resurrection.

# APRIL

## The Sacraments

---

## 1             Saint Hugh
*Bishop*

Seven loaves were placed at Christ's disposal to feed that multitude: this is the symbol of the food of the Eucharist. And they collected seven baskets of fragments. Why this number, unless, no doubt, to make us think of the seven Sacraments?

---

## 2             Saint Francis of Paola
*Confessor*

We must remember how great and how necessary the Sacraments are. It is good to remember this necessity of venerating the Sacraments, which give divine life to the faithful and were designed to give them eternal happiness!

# 3 Saint Richard

*Bishop*

The grace of Baptism is that it puts Our Lord Jesus Christ into our hearts. Now Our Lord is Heaven, which is God. Putting Heaven into the hearts of children is something essential, so that they might grow in their love of Jesus.

# 4 Saint Isidore

*Bishop and Doctor*

The Holy Ghost took possession of your hearts and souls at Baptism. But now you have grown up. Our Lord wanted you to have Confirmation, a fullness of the Holy Ghost, so as to be able to confront the difficulties that you will encounter in living out your Christian life, and finally to arrive at the destination for which you were created: Heaven, paradise, eternal life.

# 5 Saint Vincent Ferrer

*Confessor*

The Sacrament of Confirmation is nothing but the confirmation of the grace that you received at Baptism. But as you grow older, you find yourselves in conflict with all those who want to snatch this blessing away from you and to make sure that you are no longer children of God. Then Confirmation comes to "confirm" or strengthen this grace; consequently, over the course of your life, you will have to wage combat. You will have to be soldiers and fight.

---

# 6       Saint Celestine

*Pope*

"When you receive the Holy Ghost, you will be My witnesses in the world," Our Lord says in the Acts of the Apostles. Therefore we receive the Holy Ghost not only to sanctify us, but also to sanctify others, and consequently we must be witnesses to Our Lord Jesus Christ. No sooner had the twelve disciples received the Holy Ghost than they became genuine Apostles.

---

# 7       Saint Donatus

*Martyr*

Through the Sacrament of Confirmation, a baptized person also becomes a missionary. No one has the right to say: "As long as I am a good Christian and go to Heaven, it makes no difference to me if others don't go there." The Sacrament of Confirmation gives this missionary spirit, this desire to sacrifice oneself for others.

## 8 Saint Albert
*Bishop*

We need to recall that we, too, have received the Sacrament of Confirmation. In all the difficulties that the Church is going through, we need this light and this strength that the Holy Ghost gives us by His graces, so as to stay Catholic and to remain faithful to the Church of all ages.

## 9 Saint Marcellus
*Bishop*

Say in your hearts, in your consciences: "May the Holy Ghost come into me, may He fill me with His gifts so that I may be more like Our Lord." This is what we must ask in order to prepare ourselves for the combat of Christian life, because, ultimately, we know that Christian life is a continual struggle. Our Lord told us so. We must fight in order to gain the crown of Heaven, in order to win the victory and to attain everlasting life.

## 10 — Saint Fulbert
*Bishop*

"I believe, I believe in God, I believe in Our Lord Jesus Christ, I believe in the Holy Ghost, I believe in the forgiveness of sins, I believe in Holy Church, I believe in the resurrection." You will say all these things. You will say them to the world's face, and from now on let this be a law for you: that you profess your faith without fear, without apprehension, wherever you are. This is what the Sacrament of Confirmation will give to you.

## 11 — Saint Leo the Great
*Pope, Confessor, and Doctor*

This Sacrament of Penance is so beautiful, so consoling: the confession of our sins so as to have absolution personally in the sight of God! We approach the good Lord; we receive graces that help us to avoid anything that may separate us from

God personally. This is truly a personal relationship with Him.

## 12 Saint Julius
*Pope*

"Confession makes no difference. And then there are obstacles, right?" The devil is always trying to make trouble in souls; he does not like peace. The devil likes anxiety, scruples, anything that can disturb souls and deprive them of their peace. As soon as he realizes that he can introduce trouble into a soul, then he prepares to make her believe things that are not true, and exaggerate things that are simple, and then the conscience is troubled. Do not let yourselves be drawn in by these temptations of the devil.

## 13 Saint Hermenegild
*Martyr*

Remain at peace, ask the good Lord to show you correctly to what extent you are guilty, to what extent you are not guilty, and then it is necessary to tell your sins in Confession quite simply as they are, that is all. You are not telling them to the priest in Confession, but to Our Lord Himself: He is the one to whom we confess.

---

# 14

## Saint Justin

*Martyr*

The priest is only an instrument representing Our Lord, and by his absolution he washes the soul in the blood of Our Lord Jesus Christ. He is the dispenser of this blood, because we were redeemed by the blood of Our Lord and through it our sins are washed away. Because Our Lord poured out His blood, by His redemption, by His will to redeem all human beings, the priest can give absolution and therefore take sins away from souls and consciences.

---

# 15

## Saint Maximus

*Martyr*

You must not remain with a sin on your conscience because of fear, self-love, or shame; we are all sinners in God's sight; we all have sin, more or less. The priest says so at the moment of the Offertory: "My God, I offer you this sacrifice *pro innumerabilibus peccatis meis, pro innumerabilibus*

51

*negligentiis meis*, for my countless sins of commission and omission." We know very well that we are all like that.

---

# 16        Saint Bernadette
*Virgin*

We should have no apprehension, then, no fear to say quite simply in the presence of the good Lord what happened to us. The good Lord, in the Gospel, showed us His mercy, His goodness, His condescension, His love for sinners; God knows that He has shown it in all sorts of ways, right? How many examples in Scripture, in the Gospel, in which we see God's great mercy!

---

# 17        Saint Anicetus
*Pope, Martyr*

Our Lord is still merciful; it is still the same Lord who was in Palestine and had pity on sinners, who now is in the confessional when you make your confession, who is in the Holy Eucharist. It is still the same Lord, still just as merciful, still just as good. Therefore it is important to make a good confession.

# 18 Saint Placidus
*Martyr*

God requires considerable humility of us in asking us to confess our sins to a creature like ourselves, but vested with His powers, with His Holy Ghost in order to wipe them away. We are expected to present ourselves with humility in order to receive the Sacrament of Holy Eucharist, too. We must kneel down and receive the Sacred Body of Jesus on our tongue. Our Lord consequently asks us to humble ourselves. This is the spirit of the Catholic Church, the spirit of Our Lord Jesus Christ.

---

# 19 Saint Emma
*Widow*

The Good Lord is waiting for us to make a small gesture, a gesture of desire, of generosity, and then He gives us His grace, He helps us, He helps us yet a little more, and still more, above all by Holy Communion. This is the most perfect means of being united to God. In this Sacrament, we have Our Lord in us. Well, then, it is up to us to ask Him to take up all the room. It is up to us to say this to Him, to make our desire known to Him.

---

# 20             Saint Marcellinus

*Bishop*

There is a very close connection between the Sacrifice of the Mass and the Sacrament of Matrimony, because the Sacrament of Matrimony is destined to multiply the elect of Heaven, to multiply those who will be marked by the blood of Our Lord.

We spent several years of peaceful family life with good, deeply Christian parents. Every morning, my parents went to the parish church to receive Communion and attend Mass.

---

# 21             Saint Anselm

*Bishop, Confessor, and Doctor*

Our Lord wanted the Sacrament of Matrimony to be a Sacrament that represents Our Lord's nuptials with His Church. Where did this marriage, so to speak, of Our Lord with His Church take place? On the cross. Therefore Christian spouses should understand that the graces of the Sacrifice of the Mass must sanctify their marriage.

# 22 Saints Soter and Caius

*Popes and Martyrs*

The characteristics of the Sacrament of Matrimony are unity and indissolubility; in other words, there is only one love and it cannot be broken.

In the villages which have still preserved their ancient character, we see first the spire and all the houses around it; you would say that the inhabitants crowded around the village in order to be as close as possible to the altar.

# 23 Saint George

*Martyr*

The Christian family is very important. Without the Christian family, there will be no more vocations. Without vocations, what will become of the Church? Alas, we are finding out today. The fact that faith is diminishing in homes, the fact that love of Our Lord is disappearing, little by little, from homes that once would have been

Christian and deeply believing, results in the disappearance of vocations.

## 24      Saint Fidelis of Sigmaringen
*Martyr*

It is necessary to state—and I am happy to be able to do so in the presence of all my relatives gathered here, and in particular those who are joined by ties of marriage—that if a vocation is born in a family, it is generally because the family is deeply Christian. The good Lord makes use of natural means in order to communicate this grace. To say that we do not owe our vocation to a great extent to our dear parents would be to disregard their piety and devotion.

## 25      Saint Mark
*Evangelist*

You give life to your children by the good Lord's grace; give them also all the benefits that you have received: the grace of Baptism, all the graces that you have received in your homes, living with your parents—may all this be handed on faithfully. This is what Our Lord intended by the family. Therefore be faithful to the tradition of your dear parents, of all our Christian families.

---

## 26     Saints Cletus and Marcellinus
*Popes and Martyrs*

These special graces are also given because of the fidelity of these families in the faith. How do they persevere in this fidelity? Through prayer and the reception of the sacraments. No one can receive special and extraordinary graces like these unless he perseveres in the spirit of prayer. It is necessary to pray. God helps those who pray. Prayer and also the reception of the sacraments.

---

## 27     Saint Peter Canisius
*Confessor, Doctor*

Then, when the storm rages, when trials begin, when the tempest arrives, these families stand fast. They are united to God, they love God, they serve Him, and consequently they react as Job did to all his trials: "My God, You have given me everything, You have taken everything away; blessed be Your holy name." These same sentiments are found in these privileged souls. But they are found there because these souls have kept the faith.

---

# 28 Saint Paul of the Cross
*Confessor*

If there is a Christian spirit in a family, it is passed down to the children. Therefore an entire civilization of the cross is transmitted through Holy Communion, the Holy Sacrifice of the Mass. The cross and the Mass: this is truly the deepest, surest, and most efficacious source of Catholic civilization, the civilization that made these Catholic countries.

---

# 29 Saint Peter of Verona
*Martyr*

When I think of all the dying persons who were visited by a true priest, a priest who came to help them to die well, to bring them the Sacrament of Extreme Unction, the consolation of Holy Communion, the viaticum... these souls were consoled and prepared to receive the grace of final perseverance.

# 30     Saint Catherine of Siena
*Virgin*

Extreme Unction is an effect of Our Lord's sacrifice, which marks us with a final anointing so that we can go to Heaven. The Sacrament of Extreme Unction prepares us to receive the true and definitive outpouring of the Holy Spirit, when we will receive our reward in Heaven.

# MAY

## The Blessed Virgin

---

## 1 Saint Joseph the Worker

If you want to come close to Jesus, go to your Heavenly Mother. Ask the help of the Blessed Virgin Mary; she will make you love Jesus as she herself loved Him and as she herself served Him.

---

## 2 Saint Athanasius
*Bishop and Doctor*

In your heart, in your soul, in your intellect, there should be no other name now than the Name of Jesus, as it was so for the Most Blessed Virgin Mary. It is not possible that she could have had some other name in her heart, in her intellect, than the Name of Jesus. Then you will be faithful to Our Lord.

# 3      Finding of the Holy Cross by Saint Helen

"*Ave Maria, gratia plena*," full of grace, completely. There was no nook where charity was lacking, where she kept something for herself, where she tried to limit her charity. May people be able to say that about us, too.

---

# 4      Saint Monica
*Widow*

The Most Blessed Virgin appears to us at the same time as a contemplative, living on God, speaking little, reflecting on every word that Our Lord said, and also intervening when she thought that she had to intervene, as at the wedding feast in Cana.

---

# 5      Saint Pius V
*Pope*

What do you think about this relationship of the Blessed Virgin Mary, who was near the cross, with her Son? She tried to investigate the thoughts of Jesus, His desires, His joys, His sufferings. Since she was filled with the Holy Ghost, the good Lord certainly gave her special graces to understand the reason why this God was hanging on the cross.

## 6          Saint Dominic Savio
*Confessor*

It is a fact that every time the Most Blessed Virgin appeared here on earth, those who had the great grace of seeing her were lost in wonder at the Blessed Virgin's splendor, her light, her radiance, her heavenly state, like the children at Lourdes or Fatima.

## 7          Saint Stanislaus
*Bishop and Martyr*

She has only one desire: to see us keep this zeal for Our Lord Jesus Christ, this zeal for our faith. This is her honor, this is all her desire, this is her whole life: that we should remain zealous for Our Lord Jesus Christ in every fiber of our soul.

# 8     Mary Mediatrix of All Graces

She left us these ringing words of the *Magnificat*, her *Magnificat* which is the Gospel of Mary. God deigned to regard her humility, and because she was humble, she was raised up to a great dignity. "*Anima mea...*": my spirit exults with joy. Mary gives thanks to God for what she received from the Holy Ghost and became the Mother of God.

---

# 9     Saint Gregory Nazianzen

*Bishop, Doctor*

Allow the Most Blessed Virgin to be with you always, everywhere you are; everywhere we are, so that we can live with our Mother. May she not be obliged to leave us because she does not want to accept what we do or what we love. This, I think, is the resolution that we should make if we want to live with the Virgin Mary and consequently fulfill the desire that the Church expressed in her prayer: "May we always have our eyes turned toward Heaven."

# 10         Saint Antoninus
*Bishop*

If we are truly faithful to the Most Blessed Virgin Mary, then we are sure of being in the truth, whatever may happen, whatever scandals may occur around us. Whatever people may tell us, whatever people may think, we remain faithful, faithful to what the Church has always believed, to what the saints have always practiced.

---

# 11         Saints Philip and James
*Apostles*

Devotion to the Most Blessed Virgin Mary is not optional, because God Himself chose her to be our Mother. No one has the right to reject his mother! He is the one who chose her, not us. He chose her to be His Mother and by that very fact to be our Mother, because she is the Mother of Jesus and Mother of the Mystical Body of Jesus.

# 12 Saints Nereus, Achilleus, Domitilla, and Pancratius

*Martyrs*

Mary is profoundly allergic to error, allergic to sin. She cannot tolerate error. Mary is for the truth, opposed to heresy; she is by nature against all that is opposed to the truth and to holiness, against all sin, whatever it may be, even the slightest venial sin, the least negligence. She is allergic to it because she wants to remain in holiness and in truth. Let us ask her to communicate this allergy to us.

# 13 Saint Robert Bellarmine

*Bishop, Doctor*

When the heart of Jesus was pierced through, so was His Mother's heart. These two pierced hearts lived only in unison, for the glory and the kingdom of God, for the kingdom of Our Lord Jesus Christ. Their hearts beat for this alone.

# 14 Saint Boniface

*Martyr*

The Most Blessed Virgin was immaculate from her conception; if she suffered so much, without having sinned, is it not fair that we should suffer, given that we have to atone not only for the sins of others, like the Most Blessed Virgin did in union with Our Lord, but also atone for our own sins? Consequently, let us gladly accept the sacrifices and sufferings that the Good Lord asks of us.

---

# 15 Saint John Baptist de la Salle

*Confessor*

The pious women who gathered around the Blessed Virgin were prostrate at the foot of the cross and wept to see Our Lord in that state. The Most Blessed Virgin is more dignified; she thinks more, she is more elevated, she sees things from a higher perspective, she sees not only external things, but all the whole interior of Our Lord, His soul, His divinity, His resplendent glory: she knows all this and that He is there for the salvation of the world.

# 16 Saint Ubald
*Bishop*

Mary was truly created by God to be our "Morning Star," to be our safeguard, our beacon in the storm and to drive out errors, the heresies that are the daughters of Satan, the father of lies. The prince of this world fears no one as much as he fears Mary.

---

# 17 Saint Pascal Baylon
*Confessor*

Could we not state an even more profound and more exact truth: Where Mary is, there is the Church? For it was through Mary that the Apostles were the founders of the Church. And Mary is not mistaken, Mary is infallible. Mary cannot sin. She is immaculate, conceived without sin. She is holy, she is perfect, she is the light of truth. And this is what she communicated to the Apostles.

# 18        Saint Venantius
*Martyr*

Mary is truly our spiritual mother. We became her children through Baptism, and we are fed by her flesh and blood in the Eucharist.

---

# 19        Saint Peter Celestine
*Pope*

If the Most Blessed Virgin Mary had a loving heart, she had it only to love Our Lord Jesus Christ and those who were attached to Him, so as to lead all souls to her Son Jesus. She lived by that love. And because she loved Our Lord, she could never offend Him, she just couldn't.

---

# 20        Saint Bernardine of Siena
*Confessor*

No creature suffered as much as the Virgin Mary, because no creature loved Our Lord Jesus Christ so much.

# 21 Saint Hospitius
*Confessor*

She is the Queen of Martyrs. Must we believe that God gives many consolations and cruel crosses to those whom He loves? Someone can be happy, happier than ever while bearing terrible crosses. This is the mystery of Our Lord's charity.

---

# 22 Saint Julia
*Virgin and Martyr*

If the Virgin Mary had not pronounced her *Fiat*, we would not have the Holy Eucharist, either. She did pronounce her Fiat, and this is why we are so blessed as to have Our Lord Jesus Christ in our tabernacles and on our altars.

---

# 23 Saint Florentius
*Martyr*

The Fathers of the Church say that Mary is the neck of the Mystical Body, that all graces pass through her; through her, in a way, the life-giving blood of Jesus passes through the Body. Well, then, how great is our need for Mary in order to be truly members of the Mystical Body of Our Lord Jesus Christ!

---

# 24    Our Lady Help of Christians

Mary appears to us as a serene person, always calm, always loving, always zealous for Our Lord Jesus Christ. She has only one love, her Divine Son. At the cross, the Blessed Virgin remained standing. Where did she get this strength of character, this strength of temperament? From her love for Jesus.

---

# 25    Saint Gregory VII

*Pope*

The Most Blessed Virgin suffered with Jesus, and can't we say, because she suffered with Jesus at the cross, that she was a missionary, too?

---

# 26    Saint Philip Neri

*Confessor*

She shared in the immense desire that Jesus had to save souls, and so her presence at Pentecost in the midst of the Apostles is due, I think, to this missionary spirit that she had. She wanted the graces of Redemption to be able to spread throughout the world.

## 27      Saint Bede the Venerable
*Doctor*

Here is what the beautiful Gospel passages teach us: the example of our good Heavenly Mother, the Most Blessed Virgin Mary: to do everything here on earth for love of the good Lord. Anything that we do not do for love of Him is worthless.

## 28      Saint Augustine of Canterbury
*Bishop*

The Blessed Virgin was definitely brief in her conversations with Bernadette, and she repeated several times: "The message to convey to souls is to pray and to do penance...." Pray and do penance.

# 29 Saint Mary Magdalene of Pazzi
*Virgin*

Look at the Virgin Mary who had only one thought, one love: her divine Son. She never thought of anything else, she never wanted or desired anything but her divine Son and His kingdom.

---

# 30 Saint Joan of Arc
*Virgin and Martyr*

We ought to be able to ask ourselves, when we are at home, in our everyday life, in our customary activity, whether the Virgin Mary would agree with us, with what we are doing, with what we are thinking, with what we are looking at, with what we love.... It is necessary to live with the Most Blessed Virgin Mary, and that way we will truly live by Heaven.

# 31 The Queenship of the Blessed Virgin Mary

The Most Blessed Virgin Mary is the mirror of Jesus Christ; therefore she must desire Our Lord's kingdom and reign with all her heart and being. And this is why she is with us; she knows us, she follows us, she wants us to continue to affirm this truth that her divine Son is King. The reason why she reigns in Heaven is because her Son is King. She is the Queen of Heaven.

# JUNE

Priestly and religious vocations

The Sacred Heart

---

| 1 | Saint Angela Merici |
|---|---|

*Virgin*

The priest's vocation consists essentially in the call of the Church confirming the desire and the aptitudes that are necessary to collaborate in the work of Redemption that was willed and accomplished by Our Lord so as to give glory to God and to save souls The future priest says to himself: "One day, I will be sent to souls to convert them, to give them this light that they need, to lead them to eternal life."

The priestly vocation is not the result of a miraculous or extraordinary call, but the flourishing of a Christian soul who is zealous for his Creator and Savior Jesus Christ with an exclusive love and shares His thirst for the salvation of souls.

# 2           Saint Blandina

*Virgin, Martyr*

We are the creatures of Our Lord Jesus Christ. He poured out His blood for us, He came to earth to sacrifice Himself for us; therefore we want to sacrifice ourselves too for Him. This is what it is to become nuns.

---

# 3           Saint Clotilde

*Queen*

In entering into religious life, you promise to strive for Christian perfection and, in order to attain it more easily, and according to the counsels of Our Lord and the counsels of the Church, you make a commitment in these three vows of poverty, chastity, and obedience.

---

# 4           Saint Francis Caracciolo

*Confessor*

The major act of our holy religion is the Sacrifice of the Mass. If we call you consecrated religious men or women, who therefore practice this virtue of religion, it is because you practice it also at the Sacrifice of the Mass through the agency of your vows and of your continual self-offering with Our Lord on the altars.

---

# 5 Saint Boniface
*Bishop and Martyr*

In religious vows there is an aspect of victim, offering, and oblation. Therefore there is a very profound resemblance between the Holy Sacrifice of the Mass and religious vows. This is why these vows are pronounced during Mass, at the Offertory, at the moment when we also offer what will become the victim of the Holy Sacrifice.

---

# 6 Saint Norbert
*Bishop*

Did God choose us to know Him better, to enter a little more into His friendship? Clearly, that is obvious! The mere fact that you are thinking about giving yourselves entirely to the good Lord in religious life is because you want to detach yourselves from the things of this world in order to come closer to God, in order to win God over!

# 7 Saint Robert
*Monk*

Even though the Church today is going through a storm, a tornado, we can be sure of this: the thing that made great saints down through the centuries is found in prayer, in the true priesthood, in the truth of the Church, in our traditional faith. The day will come when once again it will be held in honor in the Church, and I am convinced that vocations—authentic vocations to the priesthood and religious life—will come from the families.

---

# 8 Saint Medard
*Bishop*

There is nothing like the three vows of poverty, chastity, and obedience to put us into the state which facilitates our zeal for Our Lord and the service rendered by our souls to Jesus Christ Himself; they subject our whole being, both body and soul, to Our Lord Jesus Christ.

# 9 Saints Primus and Felician
*Martyrs*

Our Lord is your Creator, He is your Redeemer, He is everything for you. It is truly necessary that He be everything for you, and if that is the case, you too must be entirely for Him. This is the whole secret of religious life. This is why a nun is happy.

# 10 Saint Margaret of Scotland
*Queen*

I hope that this religious habit will be a constant lesson for you yourself and for everyone you meet, that it will be a sign of hope, the sign of your faith and of the cross of Our Lord Jesus Christ.

# 11 Saint Barnabas
*Apostle*

Religious life cannot exist or be defined without a deep relation to supernatural faith and without a close and intimate connection with the offering of Jesus on the cross and on the altar.

## 12     Saint John of San Facundo
*Confessor*

Be faithful: what then does this fidelity mean? Fidelity comes from the Latin word *fides* which means to have faith: it is perseverance in the faith, in the spirit of faith, it is the practice of the faith, not just for one day, but throughout our life.

---

## 13     Saint Anthony of Padua
*Doctor*

The reason why we love Christ, why you have become nuns, and I—a priest and bishop, is to make Him reign, in us and around us. We are essentially missionaries.

---

## 14     Saint Basil the Great
*Bishop and Doctor*

"Learn from Me, for I am meek and humble of heart." Our Lord recommends Himself in these particular qualities, and in them we find the essentials of Christian life and of religious life.

# 15 Saints Vitus, Modestus, and Crescentia
*Martyrs*

Our story, the story of our sanctification and of our soul, is ultimately the story of the love of the Heart of Jesus for us. The more we become aware of all that Our Lord suffered for us, the more our love for His Heart will grow.

# 16 Saint Francis Regis
*Confessor*

Let us ask the Most Blessed Virgin that our lives may always be directed toward the goal for which God willed that our souls be created, and that we may one day be able to share definitively in this glory of the good Lord in union with her, through the Heart of Jesus.

# 17 Saint Gregory Barbarigo
*Bishop*

Sin is opposed to charity. The more we are filled the charity, the less we can sin. Well, then, let us be filled with this charity by the Heart of

Our Lord, which beats in ours when we receive Him in the Holy Eucharist.

---

## 18 Saint Ephrem
*Deacon, Doctor*

The Feast of the Sacred Heart is the feast of merciful love. Have merciful hearts. Bend down to sinners. We are all sinners, we all need the redemption of Our Lord Jesus Christ, the blood of Our Lord Jesus Christ. Therefore you will bend down to the souls who come to you, you will treat them paternally, maternally, by listening to them, by welcoming them kindly, gently, and patiently in order to correct their faults, so as to prepare them to receive Jesus in the Eucharist.

---

## 19 Saint Juliana Falconieri
*Virgin*

If we try to delve a bit deeper into the Heart of Jesus, into that extraordinary temple filled with the Holy Ghost, we will discover the Holy Trinity there. We will discover the Father there; Our Lord Himself said so: "He who sees Me, sees the Father; My Father and I are one." In this Holy Trinity, then, there is a perfect unity of the Father, the Son, and the Holy Ghost, which we find in the Heart of Jesus.

---

## 20        Saint Silverius
*Pope and Martyr*

Over the course of our life, as the years pass, let us try to penetrate more and more into this great mystery of the love of Jesus, who desires that all the spiritual creatures that He has made should enter into and participate in His eternal life in the Holy Trinity. That is our destiny, that is the reason why God created us, but He wanted this to happen through His adorable, merciful Heart.

---

## 21       Saint Aloysius Gonzaga
*Confessor*

Since Our Lord came to earth and was crucified and His Heart was pierced, truly Christian souls have turned toward this Heart, the merciful Heart of Jesus. Certainly devotion to the Sacred Heart is above all and fundamentally devotion to the mercy of God.

## 22         Saint Paulinus

*Bishop*

The priest is, above all, made to offer the sacrifice of Redemption, so that the graces that come down from Our Lord's Heart, pierced by the lance, may be distributed by His blood.

## 23         Saint Alice

*Martyr*

Between Mary and the priest there is a profound affinity. She prepared the Victim who was to be nailed to the cross. The priest, by the words of the consecration, makes the Victim come down onto the altar. And the Victim is there, as He was on the cross.

## 24         Nativity of Saint John the Baptist

During Our Lord's passion, one gesture of His that should touch us deeply and should mark us for our whole priestly life is the gift of His Mother that He gave: "Here is your Mother." Devotion to Mary, Mother of the priesthood, is very important, because here we arrive at the very essence of the priesthood.

---

# 25 Saint William
*Abbot*

What the Church needs, what the Catholic faithful expect, are those priests of God who manifest God in their whole person, their attitude, their way of being, and their words. The good Lord does not call you for your sake alone but for all the souls to whom you will have to devote yourself through sacrifice, your prayers, and your apostolate. If you are not zealous, these souls will be lost.

---

# 26 Saints John and Paul
*Martyrs*

We cannot define the priest without sacrifice nor sacrifice without the priest. They are essentially connected. Through the Holy Sacrifice of the Mass and the sacraments, through all the teaching that he disseminates, the priest brings the faith and supernatural life, which is nothing other than eternal life.

# 27      Our Lady of Perpetual Help

A holy priest manifests the whole Catholic religion. He is the sign of the good Lord.

The influence of sacramental grace is the influence of the cross.

---

# 28      Vigil of Saints Peter and Paul

During this Holy Mass, we will pray that the good Lord may ensure that the Catholic priesthood and religious vocations continue, despite the attacks of the world and of hell against good vocations.

---

# 29      Saints Peter and Paul

*Apostles*

The priest is the channel through which the graces of Our Lord Jesus Christ come down from Heaven to sanctify us.

I want priests to be Romans, Roman Catholics, devoted to the Supreme Pontiff, to the Church's Magisterium, to the Catholic Church.

# 30   Commemoration of Saint Paul

*Apostle*

I do not think that there is any vocation that brings deeper happiness than the priesthood, even in the midst of trials, but on the condition that the priests live it fully, totally, and without mediocrity.

# JULY

Holy Mass

---

## 1      Precious Blood of Our Lord

It is vitally important to contemplate Holy Mass, that is, to contemplate Our Lord Jesus Christ on the cross and to see in this cross the summit of God's love. Our Lord can be defined as love driven to self-sacrifice, to the point of the supreme sacrifice. Our Lord demonstrated love for His Father, love of neighbor to the last drop of His blood. This has always been the principal object of the Church's contemplation.

---

## 2      Visitation of the Virgin Mary to Saint Elizabeth

"Do you want to share in My passion? Here: I give you My cross, My sacrifice; I place Myself at your disposal every day if you want in Holy Communion; you can take My flesh, eat My flesh, drink My blood, receive My grace. Do you want this?"

---

# 3         Saint Irenaeus

*Bishop, Martyr*

The only difference between the sacrifice of the cross and the Sacrifice of the Mass is that one is bloody and the other—unbloody. At the altar we do not see blood flowing. But it is the same sacrifice, it has the same value, it is the same Victim, it is the same Priest who offers Himself, it is Our Lord; it is the same thing as the sacrifice on Calvary. This is essential for us.

---

# 4         Saint Bertha

*Widow, Abbess*

The whole spirituality of the Church is there, in Holy Mass and in the cross. This is why we can say in truth that all of Christian civilization is based on the Holy Sacrifice of the Mass.

# 5      Saint Anthony Mary Zaccaria
## *Confessor*

We must have greater devotion than ever to the Holy Sacrifice of the Mass, because it is the foundation stone of our faith.

---

# 6      Saint Gervase
## *Martyr*

On the cross, Our Lord was the greatest of all men who have ever prayed, and the Sacrifice of the Mass is the greatest prayer of the Church. All the faithful are required by the Church to be intimately, profoundly associated with this prayer, adoring God, Jesus Christ, our Creator, our Redeemer.

---

# 7      Saints Cyril and Methodius
## *Bishops*

What do the Ten Commandments say, if not to love God and to love our neighbor? And now this law of love is not only written on stones. It is engraved on the sacrifice of Jesus Christ. He is the law of love and He demonstrates it on His cross.

# 8        Saint Elizabeth of Portugal

*Widow*

"*Regnavit Deus a ligno*," "God reigned through the wood," in other words, through the cross. Consequently He reigns through the Holy Sacrifice of the Mass, because the Holy Sacrifice of the Mass is truly the sacrifice of the cross. Every Mass proclaims God's victory. At every Mass that is celebrated, there is victory over sin, and every time it is a defeat for the devil.

---

# 9        Saint Procula

*Virgin and Martyr*

Since the Mass is the continuation of Our Lord's sacrifice, Satan is conquered by it. To demolish these altars is to demolish the Sacrifice of the Mass, so that the presence of Our Lord no longer exists here on earth, and souls are no longer being saved: that is his goal. Therefore we absolutely must be opposed to this demolition by the current liturgical reform, and we must resolve to keep the Mass of all times, this priceless treasure that Our Lord gave us for our salvation.

# 10     The Seven Holy Brothers
*Martyrs*

Simple folk understood this very well: they sensed that they were better off when they had attended a Holy Mass, they loved to go to attend Holy Mass, they needed it in order to be sanctified, to sanctify their family, their work, and their profession.

---

# 11     Saint Pius I
*Pope and Martyr*

The Mass is at the heart of our apostolate, because the latter is primarily supernatural, it is primarily the application of Our Lord's graces to souls. Without the sacrifice of the cross, the source of all graces, our apostolate would be in vain.

---

# 12     Saint John Gualbert
*Abbot*

In the Mass, we have everything we need for our personal prayer life, and we can draw from it all the lessons we need to live in community and to carry on our apostolate. Jesus Christ gave

Himself to the last drop of His blood for those whom He loves.

---

# 13 Saint Anacletus
*Pope and Martyr*

In this daily combat of faith in which we find ourselves involved, whether we like it or not, the Mass is at the heart of God's work of mercy.

---

# 14 Saint Bonaventure
*Bishop, Doctor*

If we want to seek perfection, we must move toward Our Lord, toward the practice of His virtues, while casting behind us all that prevents us from coming to Him. And for this purpose, the sight of the cross is a great help to us, and the sight of the living cross that is Holy Mass.

---

# 15 Saint Henry
*Emperor*

We must find in the Holy Sacrifice of the Mass the spiritual mainspring for our whole life. This should be the mark of the Society's spirituality. In all our hesitations, trials, and difficulties, we must find in it our consolation, joy, and hope: we must find everything in the Holy Sacrifice. If there is a problem, some doubt, let us seek the solution with Our Lord in the Holy Sacrifice of the Mass.

---

# 16 Our Lady of Mount Carmel

It seems to me that the Virgin Mary standing beside the cross, Our Lady of Compassion, Our Lady Co-Redemptrix, invites each one of us and every human creature who will be born into this world. She takes us by the hand, in a way, to lead us to Calvary, to make us share in the merits of Our Lord Jesus Christ.

---

# 17 Saint Alexis
*Confessor*

At Mass and in Holy Communion you can be transformed into a victim to save souls, your own first and then those that are in the world. What a beautiful ideal Our Lord has left to you!

## 18       Saint Camillus de Lellis
*Confessor*

In receiving Our Lord, we are transformed into Him; He is the one who assimilates us, who transforms us into Himself. Consequently, we become victims with Him. We must accept this spirit of victimhood, this spirit of self-offering in reparation for our sins; we must be united to Our Lord in His spirit, the spirit of expiation.

## 19       Saint Vincent de Paul
*Confessor*

Let us have this missionary spirit, at the Holy Sacrifice of the Mass and in the duties of our state in life. I can attract souls to Our Lord Jesus Christ and save them by my self-offering, by my abandonment of self to God's will in its entirety, by accepting all the sufferings that He sends me.

## 20       Saint Jerome Emilian
*Confessor*

In our daily life, for as many days as the Good Lord gives us, the Mass is truly our support, it is truly our food. What is this daily support for our souls? It is Holy Mass, it is Communion, because the Sacrament is part of Holy Mass.

# 21      Saint Lawrence of Brindisi
*Doctor*

The Holy Sacrifice of the Mass is not a simple rite that is performed today; it is an eternal reality that transcends time and has eternal consequences for the glory of God, to save souls from Purgatory and to sanctify our souls. Every Mass truly has eternal importance.

# 22      Saint Mary Magdalene
*Penitent*

When you attend the Holy Sacrifice of the Mass, you can say to yourselves: "I am with the Virgin Mary, with Saint John, *with* Mary Magdalene by the cross of Our Lord Jesus Christ," and you can ask that the blood of Jesus be poured out on your souls to save you.

## 23        Saint Apollinaris
*Bishop and Martyr*

If we truly want to practice the virtue of religion, we will succeed by being at the altar, by uniting ourselves to Our Lord. This is the most beautiful prayer that we can say: to offer ourselves with Our Lord at the altar.

---

## 24        Saint Christina
*Virgin and Martyr*

All the merits that Our Lord was able to acquire are fully sufficient to accomplish the Redemption of the world, of humanity, of all generations until the end of time. But now it will be necessary to apply them; each soul will have to apply the Redemption. How will souls be marked with His blood? Well, through the continuation of the sacrifice of the cross.

---

## 25        Saint James the Greater
*Apostle*

The Mass is the great moment of the day. It is necessary to love our Holy Mass, to live it, to live out its lessons, too. If we offer ourselves in the morning with Our Lord Jesus Christ, we must have this state of victimhood.

---

# 26 Saint Anne
### *Mother of the Blessed Virgin*

The priest lives by his Mass and makes all those around him live by it. He makes them understand that our whole lives must be a Mass, a total oblation, a continual sacrifice of ourselves, out of love for God and for our neighbor.

---

# 27 Saint Pantaleon
### *Martyr*

The lay faithful have a kind of priesthood; they too have to offer themselves personally. It is not only the priest who offers them, because they too have a soul marked by the blood of Our Lord; they too offer themselves as a victim pleasing to the good Lord. They offer their day, through their prayers and through their actions: that is the priesthood of the lay faithful.

# 28        Saints Nazarius and Celsus

*Martyrs*

By placing yourselves under the protection of Our Lady of Compassion, or Our Lady of Sorrows, you will best share in the Holy Sacrifice of the Mass, and you will truly be united to the sacrifice of the cross throughout your life.

---

# 29        Saint Martha

*Virgin*

We must be just as attached to the Holy Sacrifice of the Mass as we are to the apple of our eye, as the thing in us that is dearest, most respectable, most sacred, and most divine.

---

# 30        Saints Abdon and Sennen

*Martyrs*

If there is one effect, one good deed of Our Lord Jesus Christ that is plain to see and should be the subject of our meditations and our acts of thanksgiving to Our Lord, it is above all the Holy Sacrifice of the Mass.

# 31 Saint Ignatius of Loyola
*Confessor*

For the glory of the Most Holy Trinity, for love of Our Lord Jesus Christ, for devotion to the Most Blessed Virgin Mary, for love of the Church, for love of the Pope, for love of the bishops, the priests, and all the faithful, for the salvation of the world, for the salvation of souls, keep this testament of Our Lord Jesus Christ! Keep the Sacrifice of Our Lord Jesus Christ! Keep the Mass of all times!

# AUGUST

Charity:
"*Credidimus caritati*,"—"We have
believed God's charity"
(*episcopal motto of Abp. Marcel Lefebvre*)

---

## 1      Saint Peter in Chains

If God has loved us, will we reject His love?
He loved us in creating us, He loved us in making
us share in the life of the Holy Trinity. It is truly
the indwelling of the Holy Trinity that accomplishes in us this work of charity. God, who is
charity, cannot help giving us charity.

---

## 2      Saint Alphonsus of Liguori
### *Bishop, Doctor*

Because He is charity, God willed that charity
should overflow in a way from the Holy Trinity
and come to be poured out through the creatures

that He would create. Everything in creation is marked by charity.

# 3          The Finding of the Body of Saint Stephen

"*Caritas,*" Saint Thomas says, "*est diffusivum sui,*" in other words, charity is an element that imparts itself, that spreads. It is the gift of self.

# 4          Saint Dominic

*Confessor*

*Omnia sperat.* Despite everything, despite the difficulties, all the obstacles, all the contradictions, charity always hopes. Because true charity places its hope in God, in the One who is the source of all goods. *Omnia sperat.* Willing the good—the good of others and God's good—the truth, the glory of God, charity hopes and it has reason to hope, because it is sure and certain that its hope will be fulfilled, if not immediately, at least at a future time. "*In te speravi, non confundar in aeternum.*" "I have hoped in Thee; I shall not be put to shame forever."

104

# 5     Dedication of Saint Mary Major

We have an astonishing resemblance to the Most Holy Trinity; obviously this is only a pale image of the Holy Trinity, but just the same it truly is charity which is in us, which the Good Lord has placed in us. And this is why He created us.

---

# 6     Transfiguration of Our Lord

We must always keep in mind that this humanity shelters the divinity; only by a miracle did Our Lord Jesus Christ not always seem as radiant as He appeared on Mount Tabor during the Transfiguration. He ought to have been radiant normally and to have had a glorified body, since He had the beatific vision.

---

# 7     Saint Cajetan
*Confessor*

The charity that we have here on earth is the same as the one that we will have in Heaven. Therefore here on earth already we can truly live the eternal life. We must strive to do so. This ought to be our joy, our consolation, our strength.

---

# 8 Saint John Vianney, the Curé of Ars

In His high-priestly prayer, Our Lord asks that we have among us the love that is in Him and that He Himself may be in us. Thus, Our Lord's goal is to restore charity to us. He accomplishes this work with His Father and the Holy Ghost.

---

# 9 Vigil of Saint Lawrence

Our Lord willed to make us share in His divine nature by sanctifying grace. At the same time as sanctifying grace, the charity of God resides in us permanently. Grace is what transforms our soul in order to fill it with the charity of Christ.

---

# 10 Saint Lawrence

*Martyr*

We also can practice love for Christ in seeking to know Him, to become familiar with all His work, His thoughts and His sentiments.

# 11 Saints Tiburtius and Susanna
*Martyrs*

Our Lord came to regenerate us, to restore to us the true Life, His own Life, divine Life. Ah! If only we could understand this great mystery which the Good Lord has wrought for us, this immense love with which God has loved us!

---

# 12 Saint Clare
*Virgin*

It is important to see the concept that Our Lord has of us, the human beings that He created. He conceives of us as burning with His love, while He lives in us and we live in Him. "If you are not with Me, if you do not love Me, if you do not keep My commandments, life no longer circulates in you, and you dry up."

---

# 13 Saints Hippolytus and Cassian
*Martyrs*

Charity is the key to life, even to divine life. The marvelous thing about it is that it is spontaneous and conscious in the gift that it makes of itself. The more it disappears in giving itself, the greater it is, as opposed to the selfishness that does not give itself. The more charity gives of itself, the more life increases.

## 14          Vigil of the Assumption

The summary of Christian morality, of Christian sanctification, is charity.

## 15          Assumption of the Blessed Virgin Mary

Let us ask the Blessed Virgin that we may commend ourselves into the hands of Jesus as she did. That we may have no other love but for her divine Son; no other will but to do the will of her divine Son. Thus at the end of our days we will be sure to obtain our eternal reward.

## 16          Saint Joachim
*Father of the Blessed Virgin*

Through this submission to the will of God, we will truly be disciples of Our Lord, and we will be loved by Him, and we will prove our love.

# 17        Saint Hyacinth

*Confessor*

Unless the love of God is at the basis of the act that I perform, it does me no good at all. Hence the importance of this love of God. Let us put it in the very depths of our soul, let us set this resolution deep in our souls, to do everything for the good Lord. How I wish that you may have precisely this love for God, and that it may be deep within you! That gives serenity in life.

---

# 18        Saint Agapitus

*Martyr*

It is necessary to make sacrifices; if not, there is no love. Sacrifice is a condition for love, and Our Lord showed us this very clearly.

The cross is the source of charity; the cross is the expression of charity; it is the return we make for charity.

# 19          Saint John Eudes

*Confessor*

Our Lord willed to give Himself to us so as to communicate to us this flame that He had in Him, this flame of love, this fire of His charity. And this fire is communicated to us in the Holy Eucharist. What a wonderful thing!

---

# 20          Saint Bernard

*Abbot, Doctor*

Basically, everything that Our Lord did, this whole framework with which Our Lord surrounded the extraordinary stages of His life on earth, all this is bathed in mercy and is in fact the good Lord's mercy, His infinite mercy, because His charity is infinite, because His mercy comes from His charity.

---

# 21          Saint Jeanne de Chantal

*Widow*

Why is charity very demanding? Precisely because you must keep back nothing for yourself in order to arrive at true charity, total and complete charity. God Himself shows us the example for this: the Father "passes" entirely into the Son; He keeps nothing back for Himself. If we want to give ourselves to the good Lord, we should not keep anything back, and then we become very rich in God.

## 22 The Immaculate Heart of Mary

We need the Heart of the Most Blessed Virgin Mary to help us persevere in the faith, so as to feel this warmth of the love of Our Lord Jesus Christ for us. Since we no longer see Him before our eyes, and we see Him less and less, we need to feel that the Virgin Mary is close to us. And I think that this was why the Virgin Mary, in Fatima, asked people to pray to her Immaculate Heart.

## 23 Saint Philip Benizi
*Confessor*

How can we put this love of Christ into practice? By taking to heart all His interests. And from this we will draw our zeal for our superiors, our confreres, the faithful, the Church, the Most

Blessed Virgin, our Holy Father the Pope, and our Bishop. Our Lord loves them as other selves. We will love Him in them; we will find in them the life of Christ.

---

# 24          Saint Bartholomew

*Apostle*

We cannot praise God and then not care for our neighbor; we cannot be filled with love for God and souls and then be self-seeking.

---

# 25          Saint Louis, King of France

*Confessor*

Everything is included in love for God, in love for Our Lord Jesus Christ. Why? Because we must love in creatures what comes from God, and we must love them in order to make them go to God. We must not love creatures for themselves or for ourselves.

# 26        Saint Zephyrinus
*Pope and Martyr*

Loving one's neighbor for God's sake is the same as loving God; God is always the one whom we love in our neighbor. This is the love that Our Lord came to kindle in our hearts. He was impelled by a fire that consumed Him, the fire of zeal for His Father's glory and for the salvation of souls. We, too, must be consumed by this desire to love the good Lord with our whole heart, with our whole soul, with all our strength, and then our neighbor as ourselves, for love of God.

---

# 27        Saint Joseph Calasanz
*Confessor*

We must love our neighbor in order to bring him to God, and therefore any effort that we make apart from the path that leads him to God is not good. We should distrust any love of neighbor that does not lead him to God: it is not inspired by God.

## 28 Saint Augustine

*Bishop and Doctor*

Let us ask God often: "Lord, give me Your charity. You gave it to me through Baptism; I had the great grace of being baptized. First of all, make me keep it, so that I do not lose it through sin. Then increase this charity in me, communicate to me Your Holy Spirit, give me Your Holy Spirit."

## 29 Beheading of Saint John the Baptist

Why did the good Lord create us? So that we might be charity, love for God and for our neighbor. All the commandments are summarized in this, so that all our actions from our childhood until our death, if we want, can and should be acts of charity, obviously with God's grace.

# 30 Saint Rose of Lima
*Virgin*

It is obvious that for Our Lord, who gave all His blood for the salvation of souls, the one thing always on His mind and in His heart is saving souls! Therefore we should try, by every means possible, to help ensure that His redemption is not in vain. Then in this way, little by little, a greater intimacy, a greater love is established between souls and Our Lord.

---

# 31 Saint Raymond Nonnatus
*Confessor*

The Creed is the fulfillment, the song of the good Lord's love for us; it is the summary of God's charity for us. Every time we recite or sing the Creed, we should remember this appeal to our love, to this charity that we must have for God. Let us strive to hear this appeal, to be ever more deeply oriented toward a true love for God.

# SEPTEMBER

**The spirit of sacrifice and love
of the cross in our life**

---

## 1       Saint Giles
*Abbot*

Over the course of our life, we have to carry our cross. We cannot discover or find Our Lord Jesus Christ here on earth unless with find Him with His cross. If we find Him, Our Lord Jesus Christ places His cross on us. He did not say, "I will give you happiness here on earth." He told us: "You will have eternal life in Heaven, but first carry your cross."

---

## 2       Saint Stephen of Hungary
*King, Confessor*

The cross is like a synthesis of charity. Nothing can demonstrate the love of God for human beings and of human beings for God as much as the cross. A person can be happier than ever while having terrible crosses. This is the mystery of Our Lord's charity. The cross makes us tremble; it is not pleasant. And yet, through it we will find our happiness, our joy. This cross wipes out our sins and saves souls.

---

## 3        Saint Pius X
### *Pope*

The Most Blessed Virgin Mary and Saint Pius X gave us an example of the battle against Satan, against errors, against Modernism. *Instaurare omnia in Christo* ["To renew all things in Christ"], to commend everything into Christ's hands. The Blessed Virgin could have no other desire than the reign of her Son; likewise Saint Pius X.

---

## 4        Saint Rose of Viterbo
### *Virgin*

The cross is sacrifice: it is abandoning one's own desires, it is disciplining one's life, it is complete submission to Jesus Christ, to His glory, to His true charity, for His charity is very demanding.

# 5 Saint Lawrence Justinian
*Bishop*

The feeling of hatred for sin has its motive in love, in the theological virtue of charity; the same virtue that attracts us to the good Lord separates us at the same time from anything that may be an obstacle to that charity. We must be convinced that starting today, and for the rest of our life, there will no longer be charity without the cross.

---

# 6 Saint Eleutherius
*Abbot*

God does not ask us to do penance just because He enjoys thwarting our tendencies. The purpose of penance is to separate us from sin and to attach us to God. That is the purpose of the whole spiritual life, all the sacraments, the Mass, all spirituality, all prayers, and all the graces that we receive.

September

# 7                                      Saint Regina

*Virgin and Martyr*

Holy souls have always had a love of suffering, penance, and the cross, if only because Our Lord Jesus Christ suffered.

---

# 8                      Nativity of the Blessed Virgin Mary

The Blessed Virgin urges us to come to the cross; she is present there, she is always present at the cross. She teaches us Our Lord's cross. I think that this is where you ought to find the strength for your spiritual life and your religious life: in the cross of Our Lord, in the Holy Sacrifice of the Mass. This is where you will find all the graces you need.

---

# 9                                Saint Gorgonius

*Martyr*

All souls are destined to be victims offered in union with the most holy soul of Our Lord, who offered Himself on the cross, the oblation in view of which all souls were created. This is the mean-

ing of the Christian life, and of all spiritual life
here on earth and in eternity.

---

# 10 Saint Nicholas of Tolentino
*Confessor*

When you suffer, when you have doubts, hesitations, trials, look at Our Lord Jesus Christ. Look
at Him in His passion, look at His cross. He too
suffered. His Apostles fled and He endured it. He
courageously endured total abandonment. And
God gave Him His reward by raising Him from
the dead. Indeed He raised Himself by the power
of His divinity.

---

# 11 Saints Protus and Hyacinth
*Martyrs*

If we believe in Our Lord Jesus Christ, we
must acknowledge that we are sinners, since He
was crucified. We must therefore seek to fight
against sin and to practice virtue.

# 12     The Most Holy Name of Mary

We must venerate Our Lord's cross. We must see it everywhere around us, wear it, and spread it everywhere. The cross of Our Lord must be everywhere, because that is what affirms Our Lord's divinity.

---

# 13             Saint Amatus
*Abbot*

Our Lord's whole life was oriented toward His cross: that was the principal act for which He came to earth. As a child, Our Lord already thought about His cross and experienced some of His cross.

---

# 14        The Exaltation of the Holy Cross

Meditate before the crucifix: "What does the sacrifice of Our Lord, Holy Mass, which is the living crucifix, mean to me? What does the cross mean to me? Does the Mass have capital importance in my life?"

# 15    The Seven Sorrows of the Blessed Virgin Mary

The Feast of the Seven Sorrows of the Blessed Virgin Mary focuses on Mary, the Mother of Sorrows, relative to the Church, relative to the Mystical Body of Our Lord, not only the physical body of Our Lord as it was immolated on Good Friday, because Mary can no longer suffer today; but when she was here on earth, she suffered for the Church, she suffered for sinners, she is the Mother of sinners.

---

# 16    Saint Cornelius, *Pope,* and Saint Cyprian, *Bishop, Martyrs*

"This child will be a sign of contradiction, and a sword shall pierce your heart." This prophecy by aged Simeon caused sorrow in the heart of the Virgin Mary, at the thought that her heart would be pierced by a sword.

# 17      The Impression of the Stigmata of Saint Francis

The flight into Egypt. Certainly the Blessed Virgin must have suffered at the thought of the journey that they had to make: to flee into Egypt, a distant country, unknown to her and to Saint Joseph, long days of travel through the desert, who knows whether there might be dangers for the Child? And so on. She could not help but feel sorrow at that moment, certainly.

---

# 18      Saint Joseph of Cupertino
*Confessor*

Third sorrow of the Blessed Virgin: "Thy father and I have sought Thee sorrowing." She had been searching for Our Lord for forty-eight hours: imagine how distraught she may have been. Our Lord answered her: "Did you not know that I must be about My Father's business?" At that moment, in her sorrow, she did not understand: "*Non intellexerunt verbum istud.*"

# 19         Saint Januarius
*Bishop and Martyr*

The Most Blessed Virgin followed Our Lord as He carried His cross, and she must have suffered to see Our Lord being struck again by that band of soldiers and fall three times along the way to Calvary, wounding His knees and covered with blood. The Most Blessed Virgin could not help but suffer horribly to see her Son treated in that way.

---

# 20         Saint Eustace
*Martyr*

The Most Blessed Virgin was also considered a martyr; she was martyred by that sword of sorrow that pierced her heart. At the moment when the soldier pierced Our Lord's heart, did she not feel, as it were—she, who was still alive—her own heart pierced by the sword that pierced her Son's heart? Thus a new sorrow of the Most Blessed Virgin: the crucifixion.

September

# 21 Saint Matthew
*Apostle and Evangelist*

The descent from the cross. Tradition tells us that the disciples who were there—Saint John, Joseph of Arimathea, and several others—took Our Lord's body down from the cross and put it into the hands of His mother. Then for a while she was able to be with the body of her Son before it was placed into the tomb.

---

# 22 Saint Thomas of Villanova
*Bishop*

No doubt it was another consolation for the Most Blessed Virgin that Our Lord told her that from now on she should consider Saint John as her son. Ultimately, though, as Saint Bernard says, it is certain that she could not help comparing Saint John and Our Lord. Our Lord is God, and Saint John is only a man; that is all the difference between Heaven and earth.

# 23              Saint Linus

*Pope and Martyr*

This should be one of your meditations, to follow the Most Blessed Virgin in all her sorrows, to offer her sorrows, to offer also all your little difficulties and afflictions in union with Mary, for the salvation of the world, for the salvation of souls.

---

# 24              Our Lady of Mercy

Since we are the disciples of a Master who suffered and died on the cross, we cannot suppose that we will live without sufferings and trials, but these trials are graces, too

---

# 25             Saint Nicholas of Flüe

*Hermit and Confessor*

A person may be going through a trial, but the good Lord knows that very well; He is still present. He withdraws for a moment to leave us in the trial for a little while. Let us accept this suffering. The good Lord allows me to suffer a little;

well, then, I accept this suffering in union with His sufferings. The good Lord never abandons the souls that do not abandon Him.

---

# 26 Saints Cyprian and Justine
*Martyrs*

Let us live with Our Lord constantly, in all our difficulties, our trials, our desires: let everything be subjected to Our Lord. Let us never be caught napping and alone, when we can have the help of the One who created us, who died for us on the cross, and who comes into us (every time we receive Him) by His Body, His Blood, His human soul, and His divinity.

---

# 27 Saints Cosmas and Damian
*Martyrs*

Every time there is a trial, it is a piece of wood, a log that you place on the fire in order to stir up your love for Our Lord, and not something that puts out the fire.

## 28 Saint Wenceslaus, Prince of Bohemia

*Martyr*

Our Lord says to us: "My yoke is easy and My burden light." When carried with Our Lord, while following Our Lord, our cross becomes light—even more so, knowing that through His cross we participate in the Redemption of the world. And even if our blood has to be shed in carrying this cross, our blood will be mixed with the blood of Our Lord, and souls will be saved.

---

## 29 Saint Michael

*Archangel*

Blessed are the angels who kept inscribed on their hearts the motto: "*Quis ut Deus?*" "Who is like God?" and were not shaken during their trial.

# 30        Saint Jerome

*Doctor*

And we, too, we should adopt this spirit of oblation, of victimhood. That ought to be your spirituality, to accept sufferings, trials, difficulties in union with the Holy Sacrifice of Our Lord on the altar.

# OCTOBER

## Christer the King

---

### 1 — Saint Remigius
*Bishop, Confessor*

What does Our Lord want, if not for His redemptive sacrifice to imbue civil society? What is Christian civilization, Christendom, if not the incarnation of the cross of Our Lord Jesus Christ in the life of a whole society? This is what we call the social reign of Our Lord And therefore this is also the truth that we must preach more forcefully today, in view of liberalism.

---

### 2 — Holy Guardian Angels

Our Lord Jesus Christ manifests Himself as our King, the king of our intellects by giving us the truth, the king of our hearts and of our wills by giving us our law, our commandments, the commandments that ought to help us to act according to His holy will. This is what Our Lord Jesus Christ inspires in the souls of those who receive Him with the right dispositions.

---

# 3     Saint Thérèse of the Child Jesus
## *Virgin*

Ask the Most Blessed Virgin to have, as she did, only one love in our hearts, only one name inscribed on our hearts: Our Lord Jesus Christ. He is God. He is the Savior. He is the Eternal Priest. He is the King of all and reigns in Heaven. There is no other king but Our Lord Jesus Christ in Heaven. He is the delight of all the elect, of all the angels, of His Holy Mother, of Saint Joseph.

---

# 4     Saint Francis of Assisi
## *Confessor*

When we read the Gospel we see that between His Resurrection and His Ascension, in other words during the forty days that He spent with His Apostles, Our Lord speaks to them only about the *regnum Dei*, the kingdom of God—about His reign, since He is God. He incites the Apostles to establish the kingdom of God in the world, in souls, in families, in societies, everywhere, so as to prepare for the eternal kingdom. His kingdom is His will: it is to do His will, on earth as it is done in Heaven.

---

# 5    Saint Placidus and Companions

*Martyrs*

When Our Lord comes on the clouds of heaven, He will indeed reign over societies! And we will see what all these presidents of secular institutes will do in the presence of Our Lord coming on the clouds of heaven to judge them. We do not have the right to limit the social reign of Jesus Christ.

---

# 6    Saint Bruno

*Confessor*

Our Lord has the right to reign; no one can take this right from Him, not even the Pope. The Pope must be the first servant of Our Lord and therefore the first to fight for the reign of Jesus Christ, and to draw the whole Church along after him, with the bishops, priests, religious men and women, everyone. Now *that* is the Church.

# 7             Our Lady of the Rosary

The Most Blessed Virgin is the mirror of Jesus Christ: therefore she must desire the kingdom of Our Lord Jesus Christ with all her heart and all her being. And this is why she is with us, she knows us, she follows us, she wants us to continue to affirm this truth: her Son is King.

---

# 8             Saint Bridget
*Widow*

How did Our Lord become King? He asserted His kingship by His cross. *"Regnavit a ligno Deus."* Jesus Christ reigned by the wood of the cross. For He conquered sin, the devil, and death by His cross! These then are three magnificent victories of Jesus Christ. Some will say that this is triumphalism. Well, yes, I agree, we certainly do want the triumphalism of Our Lord Jesus Christ.

# 9        Saint John Leonardi

*Confessor*

We must be ready to suffer for the kingdom of Our Lord Jesus Christ. He no longer reigns in our societies, in our families, in ourselves. We need this kingdom of Our Lord Jesus Christ. This is the only reason for the existence of our souls, of our hearts, of humanity, of this earth, and of all God's creation: that Jesus Christ may reign, that He may bring to souls His life, His salvation, His charity, and His glory.

---

# 10        Saint Francis Borgia

*Confessor*

Our Lord said: "No, I did not come to reign in this world, but this does not mean that My authority does not extend to the world; it extends much farther than to the world, or to one nation, or to all nations; My reign extends to the whole universe."

# 11

## Maternity of the Blessed Virgin Mary

If the Most Blessed Virgin reigns in Heaven, it is because her Son is King. She is the Queen of Heaven. Therefore we want to be among those who on earth have declared the reign of Our Lord Jesus Christ so as to be able to share also someday in His reign in Heaven for eternity.

---

# 12

## Saint Wilfrid
*Bishop*

We must do everything possible so that Our Lord Jesus Christ reigns in us personally, in our intellects; we must oblige, that is to say, submit our intellects to the kingship of Our Lord Jesus Christ; we must have in our intellects the truths that He had in His human intellect and meditated on, we must have in our wills the same desires as Our Lord, the desire to serve the Father, to do the Father's will.

# 13  Saint Edward, King of England
*Confessor*

The Blessed Virgin assures us that at the end of this struggle, "My Immaculate Heart will triumph." The Blessed Virgin will have the victory. She will triumph over the great apostasy, the fruit of liberalism. One more reason not to twiddle our thumbs! We must fight more than ever for the social reign of Our Lord Jesus Christ.

# 14  Saint Callistus I
*Pope and Martyr*

Our Lord asks that His kingdom may be established on earth as it is in Heaven. We can understand that only in this way: that His kingdom may be as perfect as possible, because in Heaven His kingdom is absolute, perfect; everyone is subject to Our Lord—that is obvious! Well, when He asks for the same thing on earth, this is because it is necessary to aim and to work to make this kingdom of Our Lord as perfect here on earth as it is in Heaven; this is what He asks, what He asks us to repeat very often, to ask the good Lord every day.

# 15          Saint Teresa of Avila

*Virgin*

What a consolation, what a support in our life here on earth to acknowledge and to extend the kingship of our beloved Savior! While this kingship is diminished more than ever today—curtailed, misunderstood, despised even by those who are responsible for proclaiming it—it is a distinguished grace to be, in this perverse world, an echo of the voice of the archangels, the angels, the apostles, the martyrs, and the confessors: "The Virgin has brought forth the King whose name is everlasting."

---

# 16          Saint Hedwig

*Widow*

Our strength is in these words of Our Lord Jesus Christ, who said: "I will be with you all days, even to the consummation of the world" (Mt 28:20). Strengthened by our union with all the elect in Heaven and with all the Catholics on earth, we are assured of victory. We do not seek to proclaim victory over those who bear a grudge against us, over those who persecute us. No, I am speaking about Our Lord's victory over Satan, a victory that He won by His cross.

---

# 17 Saint Margaret Mary Alacoque
*Virgin*

"All power is given to Me in heaven and on earth." All human beings will come before the judgment seat of Jesus Christ. He said so, and it is only to be expected. God took the trouble to come among us; this Person, in a human body and a soul, who worked among the Apostles and was born from the womb of the Virgin Mary, is obviously Heaven on earth. This Person therefore must have all authority; it cannot be otherwise.

---

# 18 Saint Luke
*Evangelist*

What do we say every day in the Our Father? "Thy kingdom come, Thy will be done on earth as it is in Heaven." What is this kingdom? There will be no peace on this earth except in the kingdom of Our Lord Jesus Christ. Because His kingdom is precisely the kingdom of these principles of love which are God's commandments. They bring society into an equilibrium and cause justice and peace to reign in it.

---

## 19      Saint Peter of Alcantara
*Confessor*

"You shall adore one God and love Him perfectly." All creation depends on this First Commandment, and all persons and all societies, being creatures of God, must submit to it, even civil societies. Everything must contribute to this love and nothing should oppose it. The kingdom of God that Our Lord came to reestablish is nothing but this kingdom of love.

---

## 20      Saint John Cantius
*Confessor*

Faith is giving to Our Lord Jesus Christ the place that is due Him in our world, in our souls, in our hearts, in our intellects, in our families, in States; it is duly making room everywhere for Our Lord Jesus Christ, who by His very nature is Savior, Priest, and King.

# 21            Saint Hilarion

*Abbot*

It is necessary to rebuild the ruined fortresses, reconstruct the bastions of the faith: first the Holy Sacrifice of the Mass of all times, which makes saints, then our chapels which are our true parishes, our monasteries, our large families, our businesses which are faithful to the social teaching of the Church, our politicians who have resolved to pursue the policy of Jesus Christ: all this is a fabric of Christian social life, of Christian customs, of Christian reflexes, which we must restore, on the scale that God wills, and when God wills.

---

# 22            Saint Mary Salome

*Martyr*

The Church, reflecting the teaching of Our Lord, has always taught that Jesus Christ is King. Therefore it was necessary to do everything possible for Him to reign on earth; of course, not in His own person, for He said, "My kingdom is not of this world." That did not mean that He was not king of the world. It meant that He had another kingdom, a kingdom that is universal and not

October

only over one State, as the Jews thought, imagining that Our Lord would be the King of the Jews.

---

## 23     Saint Anthony Mary Claret
*Bishop*

Until Vatican II . . . seeking the social reign of Our Lord Jesus Christ among nations was part of Church teaching; we were supposed to do everything we could for this intention: pray, preach, act, so as to try make Our Lord reign publicly in Catholic nations; this went without saying and this is the teaching of the Church of all times.

---

## 24     Saint Raphael
*Archangel*

All the divine attributes which we recognize from theology—God's omnipotence, His omnipresence, His permanent and supreme causality with regard to every created thing, to everything that exists, since He is the source of being—they all apply to Our Lord Jesus Christ Himself. He therefore is almighty in His power over all things, by His own nature He is King, king of the universe, and no creature, individual, or society can escape from His sovereign power and His sovereign grace.

---

## 25 Saints Chrysanthus and Daria
*Martyrs*

Our Lord wants souls to be saved—indirectly, no doubt, but effectively—through a Christian civil society which is fully subject to the Gospel, which lends itself to His redemptive plan and is the temporal instrument thereof. Consequently, what is more just, more necessary than civil laws that are subject to the laws of Jesus Christ and sanction those who transgress the laws of Our Lord in the public and social domain by imposing penalties on them?

---

## 26 Saint Evaristus
*Pope and Martyr*

This century of apostasy belongs to Jesus Christ, no doubt in a different way from the centuries of faith: on the one hand, the apostasy of a majority manifests the fidelity of the minority. On the other hand, as Church history testifies, every age of crisis prepares the way for an age of faith and a genuine renewal in fidelity to Tradition.

---

## 27            Saint Sabina

*Martyr*

Ah! If only those who govern us understood that they must be subject to Our Lord who is the King of kings: "*Rex regum, Dominus dominantium*"! He is the King, even though He does not reign today publicly as He could have done. Indeed, He could have been the King of earth and continued to rule us. But He will be that someday when He descends on the clouds of heaven, and then the whole world will have to give an accounting to this king and judge. But why not subject ourselves to Jesus Christ right now?

---

## 28            Saints Simon and Jude

*Apostles*

Our whole Society is at the service of this King; it knows no other. It has no thought, love, or activity except for Him, for His kingdom, His glory, and the accomplishment of His redemptive work on earth.

# 29          Saint Narcissus
*Bishop*

We want Our Lord Jesus Christ to reign. You just sang: "*Christus vincit, Christus regnat, Christus imperat!*" ["Christ conquers, Christ reigns, Christ commands!"] Are these just words? Mere eloquence, lyrics? No! This must be a reality. It is not impossible, or else we would have to say that the grace of the Holy Sacrifice of the Mass is no longer grace, that God is no longer God, that Our Lord Jesus Christ is no longer Our Lord Jesus Christ. We must place our trust in His grace, for He is all-powerful.

# 30          Saint Germain
*Bishop*

We believe in the kingship of Jesus Christ. We want it for ourselves personally, for our families, for our cities. Our Lord has the right to reign over us. He reigns in eternity, but He must reign here on earth too. Do we not recite every day: "Thy kingdom come, Thy will be done, O Lord Jesus Christ, on earth as it is in Heaven"? Well, then, if His kingship is supposed to be as beautiful, as

October

great here on earth as it is in Heaven, what more can we desire?

---

# 31 Saint Quentin

*Martyr*

Let us contemplate the loving act that was creation, and let us strive to realize in ourselves and around us this reign of God and of Our Lord. In order to reestablish it, God agreed to die on the cross, demonstrating once again His infinite love for disordered, sinful creatures.

# NOVEMBER

The Four Last Things:

Heaven, Purgatory, Hell, death

---

## 1                          All Saints

My dear friends, don't you see between this official recognition of the Society and the Feast of All Saints an extraordinary mystical connection which corresponds perfectly to the purpose of the Society of Saint Pius X? It is part of its very essence to seek sanctity, not only to seek holiness but to make holy things. On this beautiful day of All Saints, I am sure that the angels rejoice to see the recognition of this Society, which is designed to make holy priests who will communicate holiness to the faithful.

# 2                                 All Souls' Day

If we want to be conformed to the spirit of the Catholic Church, we must have a real devotion to the souls in Purgatory, the place where we ourselves will most likely stay for a more or less long time, let us hope: this will be the sign of our election.

---

# 3                                    Saint Hubert
*Bishop*

No doubt, souls can go directly to Heaven. But we know all too well that we are sinners and that we all have to be purified in this anteroom of Heaven so as to dress our souls, in a way, so that they may be pure and perfect to meet the One who is Truth, Beauty, and Perfection.

---

# 4                          Saint Charles Borromeo
*Bishop*

Why Purgatory? Because we must enter Heaven in the most perfect purity. It is inconceivable that souls could enter into the vision of God, a union that surpasses all that we can imagine, and enter into divinity itself, share in God's light, while having within them dispositions that were contrary to this light, contrary to this glory, to this purity and this holiness of God.

# 5 Saint Elizabeth, Mother of Saint John the Baptist

If we could only know the holiness and the incomparable purity of God, we would not be surprised that He discovers in us imperfections that are not suited to the holiness of the Trinity.

# 6 Saint Leonard

*Bishop*

We must meditate on this reality of Purgatory, be united to the souls of our brethren, to the souls of our relatives, to the souls of our departed friends, and to the souls of that countless multitude of deceased persons who have no one among their acquaintances to pray for them. This is a duty for us; these souls are suffering and expect their deliverance from us.

# 7                      Saint Florentius

*Bishop*

We should offer sacrifices for the souls in Purgatory and also benefit from the treasury that the Church places at our disposal, the treasury of the merits of the saints, of all those who went before us on earth. The Church has a treasure of merits that she can place at the disposal of souls who are willing to apply them for the souls in Purgatory.

---

# 8    The Four Holy Crowned Martyrs

*Martyrs*

Let us have great respect for the bodies of those who have been sanctified, and we should bury them as Christians have always done. The veneration of our cemeteries and the maintenance of the graves of our faithful departed should always be perfect, so that we demonstrate in this way the faith that is ours: we believe that these bodies will one day rise again.

# 9      Dedication of the Basilica of Saint John Lateran

This is the cathedral where the man who is elected by the priests of Rome to be the Bishop of Rome comes to take possession of his cathedral and his see. God, who guides all things in His infinite wisdom, prepared Rome to become the See of Peter and the center of the dissemination of the Gospel.... If we investigate how the ways of Providence and of the divine wisdom pass through Rome, we will conclude that one cannot be Catholic without being Roman.

---

# 10      Saint Andrew Avellino
### *Confessor*

We have good reason to believe that our sojourn here on earth is an ephemeral stay, a transitory stay. When I think of those whom I was able to meet as a child, where are they now? I think that three quarters of the human beings who were alive when I was a child are no longer on this earth. Others have replaced them, and so it is through all the ages. Where are all those souls?

# 11 Saint Martin
*Bishop*

Reflect that what is spiritual is infinitely more alive, more real than what is material. The material world came from the spiritual world, and everything will be resolved into the spiritual. Therefore what we do not see is more real than what we see.

# 12 Saint Martin I
*Pope, Martyr*

What is our goal? The goal is to have us return to the Holy Trinity. That is the promised land! The promised land is the Holy Trinity: it is Heaven, Heaven is God, God is the Holy Trinity.

# 13 Saint Didacus (or Diego)
*Confessor*

Heaven is the Father; Heaven is God. It is not a place where the Father resides. It is the Father Himself. In the Apocalypse, Saint John tells us so: "I saw no temple," there will be no place. God will be in us, therefore God is Heaven.

# 14        Saint Josaphat
*Bishop and Martyr*

It is necessary to meditate on Heaven, we should think about it often. No doubt, you will say to me: "Why not talk about the Last Things? You speak only about Heaven, but Purgatory and Hell exist, too." I think that it is an excellent thing to speak about Hell on retreats. But I think that it is also very useful to speak about Heaven, especially for souls that have been called and chosen by the good Lord, since they have already lived with the desire for sanctification.

---

# 15        Saint Albert the Great
*Bishop, Doctor*

It seems to me that the important thing, during the years which the good Lord gives us to live, is not to have forty, fifty, sixty, seventy, or more of them to live here on earth; the essential thing is to live them well, to use them in such a way that our years sing the glory of the Lord, carry out the will of God for us, and allow us someday to share in eternal life.

November

# 16 Saint Gertrude
*Virgin*

If we suffer, if we weep, if we are persecuted, if we are in anguish, in difficulties, what keeps us going is hope: this hope is Heaven. Therefore it is the hope of belonging to God completely, for all eternity.

# 17 Saint Gregory the Wonderworker
*Bishop*

Hope is having your sights set on the eternal goods. The good Lord gave us a soul which needs Him, which needs eternal goods. We should therefore live out our pilgrimage here on earth with our eyes turned toward Heaven.

# 18 Dedication of the Basilicas of Saint Peter and Saint Paul

Our Lord, who is all charity, has only one desire, and that is to bring us to the place where there will be nothing but charity, where there will no longer be anything contrary to charity. And that is Heaven. Well, then, let us seek to be united more and more to Our Lord Jesus Christ so as to be filled with His charity and thus prepare our Heaven.

## 19 Saint Elizabeth of Hungary
*Widow*

It is frightening to think that everything Our Lord, our God, did for us might be in vain, that there might be no response to that love. Consequently we understand that God's justice allows and wills that those who reject His love should not enjoy it for all eternity. This is a dreadful prospect, but God can do nothing about it, since man himself is the one who blocks the way to God's love in him and secludes himself in his selfishness, in his pride, rejecting all light.

## 20 Saint Felix of Valois
*Confessor*

I would say that we want to experience a bit of Heaven already, since we are made to go to Heaven. It is indeed necessary for us to prepare for it here on earth. Therefore it is necessary to create this atmosphere of the reign of Our Lord Jesus Christ, since we will find it when we die.

# 21 Presentation of the Blessed Virgin Mary

"Thy will be done, on earth as it is in Heaven," and not "my will be done." This is the spirit in which we should live in order to follow Our Lord Jesus Christ and to arrive at the gates of Heaven which will be open to us.

# 22 Saint Cecilia
*Virgin and Martyr*

Thus we can suppose that Heaven is something that will delight us; it will be so beautiful, so splendid, so moving that we will be ecstatic for joy and happy to draw near to the One who is our God. To draw near to God is to draw near to the Light, it is to draw near to charity, it is to draw near to Love. It is quite difficult for us to imagine these things, yet that is the reality, and all that we can know about Heaven makes us hope that one day we too will go to join those who are there and enjoy eternal happiness.

# 23                    Saint Clement

*Pope and Martyr*

We are assured that we too, someday, will have the joy of the resurrection, if however we follow Our Lord, if we love Him, like the Virgin Mary standing by the cross.

---

# 24             Saint John of the Cross

*Doctor*

Let us try to delve more and more into this great mystery of the love of Jesus, who wills and desires that the spiritual creatures that He has made should share in His eternal life in the Holy Trinity.

---

# 25      Saint Catherine of Alexandria

*Virgin and Martyr*

Our inheritance will be to dwell in the Father's house; this is the almost private abode of the Holy Trinity; finally we will enter truly into the bosom of the Trinity, instead of resting so to speak outside of God, if I may say so, like infants who died without Baptism.

# 26          Saint Sylvester
*Abbot*

We must do everything possible not to hinder our hearts from being oriented toward Heaven. We would have to be able to say to ourselves: "What would the Most Blessed Virgin Mary think if she was truly present by me, aware of everything that I say, everything that I think, everything that I love?" Consider allowing the Most Blessed Virgin Mary to be with you always, wherever you are.

---

# 27          Our Lady of the Miraculous Medal

In Heaven and at the Last Judgment, we will be judged solely on this: what was our relationship and what is today our relationship with Our Lord Jesus Christ? Have we lived in union with Him, particularly in the Sacrament of the Eucharist? Have we followed His counsels? Have we spent our life under Our Lord's protection, under His influence, united with Him in our nature now transformed by grace? That is what we will be judged on.

# 28       Saint Catherine Labouré

*Virgin*

When Our Lord comes on the clouds of heaven, He will ask us: "What have you done with all that I did for you? How have you received me in My messages, how have you received My apostles, My sacrifice, My sacraments?" And what will be our response then? May it be, my beloved brothers, the one given by the Most Blessed Virgin Mary.

---

# 29       Saint Saturninus

*Martyr*

We do not have to worry so much about tomorrow. If we are truly living with God, if we have truly abandoned ourselves to Him, well, then, the good Lord will show us the path to take, day by day. The path will be made clear perhaps only twenty-four hours in advance, maybe only forty-eight hours in advance, maybe two hours in advance—we don't know. Let us leave ourselves in God's hands and so we will be certain that we are His children, subject and entirely united to Him.

# 30

## Saint Andrew

*Apostle*

The saints, the martyrs wanted to suffer, they desired the cross. Remember these words of Saint Andrew when he saw the cross: "*O bona crux,*" "O good cross." Saint Andrew knew that, nailed to the cross, He would resemble Our Lord more, that he would go up to Heaven, and that by sharing in His sufferings, he would save souls.

# DECEMBER

**The mystery of Our Lord Jesus Christ:
the Incarnation**

---

## 1       Saint Elias
*Bishop*

The season of Advent, during which the
Church recalls the three comings of Our Lord (the
Incarnation, His presence in the souls of the just,
and the end of the world), is redolent with the
thought and presence of the Most Blessed Virgin.
Indeed, is it possible to prepare for the feast of
the Nativity without being in the presence of the
woman from whom the Word of God was to be
born?

---

## 2       Saint Bibiana
*Virgin and Martyr*

What were the thoughts of the Virgin Mary
concerning her Son? Isn't the Gospel of Saint John
the Gospel of the Blessed Virgin? For years Saint

John watched over the Virgin Mary. They were able to converse together at length, and the Virgin is certainly at the origin of the magnificent reflections of his Gospel, particularly of its wonderful prologue.

---

## 3 Saint Francis Xavier

*Confessor*

Was it the temporal generation [of Christ] that occupied the Virgin Mary's thoughts? It seems not. The Gospel of Saint John speaks on the contrary about the divine generation of Jesus Christ. He relates the eternal birth: "*Deus erat Verbum.*" "The Word was God."

---

## 4 Saint Peter Chrysologus

*Bishop, Doctor*

"From God I proceeded and came. For I came not of Myself, but He sent Me" (Jn. 8:42). These terms: came, proceeded, sent, signify the same mission, which presupposes an eternal procession in God. The Word can be sent by the Father since He proceeds from Him. His temporal mission has His eternal procession as its root.

## 5           Saint Sabbas

*Abbot*

The perfect unity of the Father and the Son is an actual reality, belonging to the present. "I and the Father are one" (Jn. 10:30). Only the Son who is always immanent to the Father can speak this way and say: "I am not alone, because the Father is with Me" (Jn. 16:32). All the actions performed by Our Lord are truly divine; they were done by the Word Himself.

## 6           Saint Nicholas

*Bishop*

Our Lord is "more" God than man. Of course, He is perfectly man. He is even the most perfect of all men, but, all the same, the one who gives subsistence to His humanity is God. The Word of God is the one who assumes this humanity.

## 7           Saint Ambrose

*Bishop and Doctor*

The fact of being born in the womb of the Virgin Mary does not affect His Person. Since Our

Lord's Person is divine, it is eternal, it does not enter into time and is not affected by the changing of temporal things. See what a great mystery the Incarnation is!

---

# 8      Immaculate Conception of the Blessed Virgin Mary

"*Tota pulchra es, Maria, et macula originalis non est in te.*" "You are all-beautiful, Mary, and there is no original sin in you." If the Most Blessed Virgin Mary was immaculate in her conception, the reason was because she had to bear in her womb Our Lord, the Son of God, because she had to give Him to the world, because she had to live with Him and be His Mother.

---

# 9      Saint Valerie

*Virgin and Martyr*

A second birth which we must contemplate in Our Lord is His birth as man: "*Et homo factus est.*" ["...and was made man."] "*Verbum caro factum est.*" ["The Word was made flesh."] Our Lord was born here on earth. He willed it: He is the center, He is the heart of all human history.

# 10 Saint Melchiades

*Pope and Martyr*

Jesus is "the image of the invisible God." We like to see the persons whom we love. Now God asks us to love Him and yet He hides from us, He is invisible. So this invisible God sent His Word, His image, and He made this image in flesh and bone so that human beings could in a way touch God, see Him with their own eyes, speak to Him, and finally take His advice.

---

# 11 Saint Damasus I

*Pope*

Jesus is indeed Emmanuel, God-with-us. If this man is God, what an abundance of gifts must fill His soul and His body! God Himself took charge of this soul and this body, thus conferring on this man unique attributes, rights, gifts, and privileges surpassing anything imaginable.

# 12        Our Lady of Guadalupe
*Patroness of the Americas*

By nature and necessarily, this grace of union confers unique titles on this Person living in this human nature: Mediator, Savior, Priest, and King. All mediation, all priesthood, all kingship among creatures can only be participations in these properties, which are the jewels natural and proper to Our Lord Jesus Christ.

---

# 13      Saint Lucy, *Virgin and Martyr,* and Saint Odile, *Virgin*

To acknowledge the mission of Jesus in its full sense is to believe in the mystery of His Person, of His divine filiation, of His Incarnation, of His saving ministry.

---

# 14       Saint Nicasius of Rheims
*Bishop, Martyr*

The Word of God, the Son of God became incarnate in order to redeem us from our sins and to incorporate us into Himself, and by that very fact to restore to us our status as children of God.

## 15        Saint Valerian

*Martyr*

If a term can be found that explains to some extent the great mystery of the Incarnation and of the Hypostatic Union of the Word of God with human nature, this term is none other than charity.

---

## 16        Saint Eusebius of Vercelli

*Bishop, Martyr*

The Word of God therefore took flesh because of man's sin in order to make reparation for it and thus to cause divine live to be reborn in souls, so that they might once again be pleasing to God and glorify Him in this world and for all eternity.

---

## 17        Saint Lazarus

*Bishop*

Given man's fall from grace, in His immense mercy God decided to send His Son, the Word. And the Word was sent to take a body like ours, to be lifted on the cross, to offer His life and then to rise again from the dead so as to bring us along

December

the way the Heaven. What is more charitable than that?

---

# 18         Saint Gatian of Tours
*Bishop*

Becoming incarnate was the best way for God to demonstrate His charity and to stir us to a greater love for Him. Seeing the extent to which God loves us, we in turn are called to love Him with all our heart.

---

# 19         Saint Urban V
*Pope*

Finally, the third birth that we must consider is the birth of Jesus in our souls. I would say that this is the most important one for us, because it is the one that makes us participate in the eternal birth of God, of Jesus as Word. It is the one that makes us participate in His birth here on earth, in His sacred body, in His soul.

# 20            Saint Zenon

*Martyr*

From the Israel of the Old Testament is born the Israel of the New Testament, whose head is the Incarnate Word, forming His people and leading them through this desert so as to bring them to the Promised Land, which is none other than the Trinity Itself.

# 21            Saint Thomas

*Apostle*

The particular mission of Our Lord, the mission of the Word in the mystery of the Incarnation and in the mystery of Redemption, continues and perseveres in the Church, in priests, in the development and the combat of His Mystical Body.

# 22            Saint Honoratus

*Martyr*

When the Virgin Mary carried Jesus in her arms, it was already the whole Church that she carried. But if it is true that Mary carried Life, divine life in her arms and that she already carried us in her arms, this is because we were attached to Our Lord Jesus Christ by our Baptism, and baptized in His blood.

---

# 23          Saint Victoria

*Virgin and Martyr*

What a great mystery is this intimate union of Our Lord Jesus Christ with His Church, with His mystical Bride! He gave her everything. He gave her His life, His blood, all His gifts. And now many of those who receive these graces over the course of their life are already in eternity united with Jesus in His glory.

---

# 24          Vigil of the Nativity

To give the life of grace to souls is the purpose of the Incarnation of Jesus Christ. For no other reason did He lie in the manger, live for thirty years in Nazareth, preach the Gospel, and mount the cross, pour out His blood, and rise again: so that there might be a Church, priests, and supernatural life.

# 25        The Nativity of Our Lord

With the shepherds, let us go to the manger. There we will find the Virgin Mary carrying the Newborn in her arms. Let us try to ask the Most Blessed Virgin Mary what she is thinking. This is the eternal God whom she carries in her arms. Well, Mary must have thought that all was there in her arms: the Light of the world, the charity that comes from the Holy Trinity, the life that was to be poured out into all the members of the Mystical Body.

---

# 26        Saint Stephen

*First Martyr*

Saint Stephen was "*plenus gratia et fortitudine*," the Acts of the Apostles say, "full of grace and fortitude." Well, I think that this is an example to keep in mind! You, too, should have pure hearts and the desire to detach yourselves from all the things of this world so as to be attached to God, to Our Lord Jesus Christ.

# 27      Saint John the Evangelist
*Apostle*

Let us ask Saint John today for this special grace to believe in the love of Our Lord Jesus Christ, in the love of God. We are nothing but the effect, the consequences, the testimony of God's love for His creatures.

---

# 28      The Holy Innocents

With the shepherds, we will go to that little Child, and despite His frail appearance we will believe in His divinity, confronting all those who, on the contrary, think of doing away with the Child as soon as He is born. Herod is already sending his troops to kill all the infant boys less than two years old, hoping that this future King will be among those children. Madman! He is opposing the One who comes to save him.

# 29     Saint Thomas of Canterbury
*Bishop, Martyr*

"*Venite adoremus, venite adoremus,*" Yes, we want to adore the Infant Jesus, we want to adore God-made-man. And in so doing, to imitate first the Virgin Mary and Saint Joseph who lavished their attention on Him. With what profundity, with what awareness and faith Joseph and Mary must have adored the Infant Jesus!

---

# 30     Saint Eugene
*Bishop*

The shepherds are joined by the angels from Heaven, and soon by the magi, the "Three Kings." And year after year, the number of those who adore Our Lord would increase. There would be great joy in the world, not only among the Jews: "*Gaudium magnum annuntio vobis,*" the angels say, "I bring you tidings of great joy." Yes, they announce great joy to us.

# 31       Saint Sylvester

*Pope*

Let us ask the Most Blessed Virgin to teach us to understand the mystery of the Incarnation of Our Lord Jesus Christ and the motive for it. She heard the shepherds and the praises that they declared. *"Maria autem conservabat omnia verba haec et conferens in corde suo."* "Mary kept all these words, pondering them in her heart." This gives us an insight into the prayer life of the Most Blessed Virgin Mary. Well, let us ask her to tell us about her prayer, to tell us about the thoughts that she had.

# SOURCES

Legend:
HOMEC = Homily in Écône
CONFEC = Spiritual conference in Écône

# JANUARY

1  HOMEC 10A, January 1, 1977.
2  Homily for the Sisters, January 4, 1987.
3  Letter with season's greetings, December 31, 1980, *Pax Vobis* no. 8.
4  CONFEC 119A, January 8, 1987.
5  *Ibid.*
6  Homily for the Sisters, January 21, 1990.
7  HOMEC 6A, Christmas 1975.
8  HOMEC 44B, January 8, 1989.
9  *Ibid.*
10  *Ibid.*
11  HOMEC 6A, Christmas 1975.
12  Homily, Geneva, March 23, 1980.
13  HOMEC 10A, January 1, 1977.
14  Retreat preached to the Sisters, Quasimodo Sunday 1986, 4th conf.
15  Retreat preached to the Sisters, September 1976, 9th conf.
16  HOMEC 6A, Christmas 1975.
17  *Ibid.*
18  HOMEC 19A, October 28, 1979.
19  Homily, Saint-Joseph-des-Carmes School, March 19, 1986.
20  Letter to Members no. 3, Christmas 1977.
21  *Ibid.*
22  Letter to Members, no. 2, Christmas 1976.
23  Homily for the Sisters, March 20, 1980.
24  HOMEC 6A, Christmas 1975.
25  Letter to Members no. 2, Christmas 1976.
26  Retreat preached to the Sisters, September 1984, 12th conf.

27 *Le mystère de Jésus* [*The Mystery of Jesus*] (Clovis), p. 111.
28 *Ibid.*
29 Letter to Members no. 2, Christmas 1976.
30 Homily for the Sisters, February 11, 1990.
31 HOMEC 44B, January 8, 1989.

# FEBRUARY

1 Retreat preached to the Sisters, Quasimodo Sunday 1986, 2nd conf.
2 *La sainteté sacerdotale* [*Priestly Holiness*] (Clovis), p. 65.
3 Homily for the Sisters, February 18, 1990.
4 *Ibid.*
5 *La sainteté sacerdotale*, 167.
6 *Lettres pastorales* (Clovis), p. 137 – Conference given to the Sisters, December 2, 1975.
7 Homily for the Sisters, January 21, 1990.
8 Homily for the Sisters, February 18, 1990.
9 Retreat preached to the Sisters, September 27, 1976, 7th conf.
10 Conference given to the Sisters, November 21, 1974.
11 *La sainteté sacerdotale*, 228.
12 Retreat preached to the Sisters, Quasimodo Sunday 1986, 7th conf.
13 *Itinéraire spirituel* [*Spiritual Journey*] (Traddiffusion), p. 44.
14 Retreat preached to the Sisters, September 27, 1976, 7th conf.
15 *La sainteté sacerdotale*, 220 – Retreat preached to the Sisters, Quasimodo Sunday 1986, 2nd conf.
16 *Marcel Lefebvre* (Clovis), p. 606.
17 Retreat preached to the Sisters, Quasimodo Sunday 1986, 7th conf.
18 *Itinéraire spirituel*, 44.
19 Retreat preached to the Sisters, September 27, 1976, 7th conf.
20 *Le mystère de Jésus*, 154-155.
21 Homily for the Sisters, September 28, 1984.
22 *La sainteté sacerdotale*, 227 – *Itinéraire spirituel*, 43.
23 Retreat preached to the Sisters, September 27, 1976, 7th conf.
24 Homily for the Sisters, February 28, 1988 – Retreat preached to the Sisters, Quasimodo Sunday 1986, 3rd conf.

25 CONFEC 16A, January 27, 1975.

26 CONFEC 55B, January 16, 1978.

27 *Un évêque parle* [*A Bishop Speaks*] (DMM), pp. 15-16.

28 Homily for the Sisters, June 5, 1977.

29 *La sainteté sacerdotale*, 457 – Homily for the Sisters, September 28, 1984.

# MARCH

1 Retreat preached to the Sisters, Quasimodo Sunday 1978, 2nd conf.

2 *Le mystère de Jésus.*

3 Retreat preached to the Sisters, Quasimodo Sunday 1989, 2nd and 1st conferences.

4 Retreat preached to the Sisters, Quasimodo Sunday 1976, 5th conf.

5 HOMEC 1A, April 11, 1971.

6 Retreat preached to the Sisters, Quasimodo Sunday 1978, 4th conf.

7 Retreat preached to the Sisters, September 1976, 2nd conf.

8 Retreat preached to the Sisters, Quasimodo Sunday 1989, 2nd conf.

9 *Ibid.*

10 *Ibid.*

11 Retreat preached to the Sisters, Quasimodo Sunday 1978, 4th conf.

12 Retreat preached to the Sisters, Quasimodo Sunday 1989, 1st conf.

13 HOMEC 25B, June 19, 1982.

14 Retreat preached to the Sisters, September 1984, 6th conf.

15 HOMEC 12A, May 29, 1977.

16 Retreat preached to the Sisters, September 1976, 2nd conf.

17 *Ibid.*, 5th conf.

18 HOMEC 22A, April 10, 1981.

19 Conference given to the Sisters, November 19, 1974.

20 Retreat preached to the Sisters, September 1984, 5th conf.

21 Retreat preached to the Sisters, Quasimodo Sunday 1978, 3rd conf.

22 *La messe de toujours* [*The Mass of all Times*] (Clovis), p. 26.
23 *Ibid.*
24 Retreat preached to the Sisters, September 1984, 2nd conf.
25 *Ibid.*, 12th conf.
26 HOMEC 15A, March 26, 1978.
27 *La messe de toujours*, 72.
28 Homily for the Sisters, Notre-Dame-de-Compassion, 1989.
29 *La messe de toujours*, 156.
30 *Ibid.*, 106.
31 *Ibid.*, 26.

# APRIL

1 Homily for the Sisters, July 18, 1976.
2 HOMEC, March 31, 1983.
3 Homily for the Sisters and his family, Saint-Michel-en-Brenne, May 1, 1981.
4 HOMEC 2B, June 2, 1974.
5 HOMEC 4A, April 20, 1975.
6 HOMEC, May 30, 1971.
7 HOMEC, June 10, 1984.
8 HOMEC 28A, May 22, 1983.
9 HOMEC 12A, May 29, 1977.
10 HOMEC 5B, December 7, 1975.
11 Conference given to the Sisters, Albano, March 20, 1976.
12 Retreat preached to the Sisters, September 1984, 1st conf.
13 *Ibid.*
14 *Ibid.*
15 *Ibid.*
16 *Ibid.*
17 *Ibid.*
18 HOMEC 32B, April 4, 1985.
19 Retreat preached to the Sisters, September 1976, 5th conf.
20 Conference given to the Sisters, January 6, 1978 – *La petite histoire de ma longue histoire* [*Little Story of My Long Life*]
21 Conference given to the Sisters, January 6, 1978.
22 Retreat preached to the Sisters, Quasimodo Sunday 1988, first and only conf.; Quasimodo Sunday 1989, 10th conf.

23 Homily for the Sisters and his family, Saint-Michel-en-Brenne, May 1, 1981.

24 *Ibid.*

25 *Ibid.*

26 HOMEC 30A, April 10, 1984.

27 *Ibid.*

28 Retreat preached to the Sisters, Quasimodo Sunday 1989, 11th conf.

29 HOMEC 20B, June 27, 1980.

30 Conference given to the Sisters, January 6, 1978 – HOMEC 32B, May 25, 1985.

# MAY

1 Homily for the Sisters, Quasimodo Sunday 1981.

2 Homily for the Sisters, Quasimodo Sunday 1979.

3 Retreat preached to the Sisters, September 1974, 10th conf.

4 HOMEC 1B, December 8, 1972.

5 Homily for the Sisters, Feast of the Seven Sorrows of Our Lady, 1987.

6 HOMEC 47A, August 15, 1990.

7 HOMEC 5A, August 15, 1975.

8 HOMEC 45A, May 14, 1989.

9 HOMEC 47A, August 15, 1990.

10 HOMEC 6A, December 8, 1975.

11 Retreat preached to the Sisters, September 1984, 12th conf.

12 HOMEC 45A, May 14, 1989.

13 HOMEC 8B, August 22, 1976.

14 Retreat preached to the Sisters, September 1976, 9th conf.

15 Retreat preached to the Sisters, September 1984, 1st conf.

16 *Lettres pastorales* (Clovis), p. 215.

17 HOMEC 45A, May 14, 1989.

18 *Itinéraire spirituel*, 75.

19 HOMEC 8B, August 22, 1976.

20 Homily for the Sisters, September 29, 1978.

21 *Ibid.*

22 HOMEC 8A, June 17, 1976.

23 Homily for the Sisters, Quasimodo Sunday 1982.

24 Homily for the Sisters, February 9, 1986.

25 Homily for the Sisters, Feast of the Seven Sorrows of Our Lady, 1987.

26 *Ibid.*

27 Homily for the Sisters, February 9, 1986.

28 Homily for the Sisters, February 11, 1990.

29 HOMEC 38A, April 4, 1987.

30 HOMEC 47A, August 15, 1990.

# JUNE

1 *La sainteté sacerdotale*, 191.

2 Homily for the Sisters, Quasimodo Sunday 1977.

3 HOMEC 37A, September 29, 1986.

4 Retreat preached to the Sisters, September 1984, 11th conf.

5 *Ibid.*

6 Retreat preached to the Sisters, Quasimodo Sunday 1986, 4th conf.

7 HOMEC 4B, June 29, 1975.

8 Homily for the Sisters, March 20, 1980.

9 Conference given to the Sisters, December 12, 1975.

10 Homily for the Sisters, March 30, 1975.

11 Constitutions of the Congregation of Sisters

12 HOMEC 6A, December 8, 1975.

13 Retreat preached to the Sisters, Quasimodo Sunday 1986, 5th conf.

14 Conference given to the Sisters, October 24, 1990.

15 Homily for the Sisters, June 2, 1989.

16 *Ibid.*

17 HOMEC 17B, Easter 1979.

18 HOMEC 31B, June 29, 1984.

19 Homily for the Sisters, June 2, 1989.

20 *Ibid.*

21 Retreat preached to the Sisters, Quasimodo Sunday 1989, 1st conf.

22 HOMEC 21A, September 20, 1980.

23 *La sainteté sacerdotale*, 288-289.

24 *Ibid.*, 293.

25 *Ibid.*, 11.
26 *Ibid.*, 191 and 300.
27 *Ibid.*, 12 – HOMEC 13A, September 18, 1977.
28 Homily, Le Bourget, November 19, 1989.
29 Homily, Lausanne, July 9, 1978 – Conference, Tourcoing, January 30, 1974.
30 Pious thought reprinted from a prayer card commemorating the ordination of a priest.

# JULY

1 *La messe de toujours* [*The Mass of All Times*] (Clovis), p. 155.
2 Conference given to the Sisters, January 6, 1978.
3 Retreat preached to the Sisters, Quasimodo Sunday 1989, 10th conf.
4 Retreat preached to the Sisters, September 1984, 11th conf.
5 HOMEC 13A, September 18, 1977.
6 *La sainteté sacerdotale*, 208.
7 *Ibid.*, 214.
8 Retreat preached to the Sisters, Quasimodo Sunday 1978, 3rd conf.
9 Retreat preached to the Sisters, Quasimodo Sunday 1989, 10th conf.
10 Conference given to the Sisters, January 6, 1978.
11 *La sainteté sacerdotale*, 386.
12 Retreat preached to the Sisters, Quasimodo Sunday 1978, 7th conf.
13 Retreat preached to the Sisters, Quasimodo Sunday 1989, 10th conf.
14 Retreat preached to the Sisters, September 1976, 5th conf.
15 Retreat preached to the Sisters, Quasimodo Sunday 1978, 7th conf.
16 *La messe de toujours*, 147.
17 *La sainteté sacerdotale*, 212-213.
18 Retreat preached to the Sisters, Quasimodo Sunday 1989, 11th conf.
19 Retreat preached to the Sisters, Quasimodo Sunday 1978, 3rd conf.

20 Retreat preached to the Sisters, Quasimodo Sunday 1989, 11th conf.

21 CONFEC 85A, March 23, 1981.

22 *La messe de toujours*, 147.

23 *Ibid.*, 149.

24 Conference given to the Sisters, January 6, 1978.

25 Retreat preached to the Sisters, Quasimodo Sunday 1978, 7th conf.

26 *La sainteté sacerdotale*, 387.

27 Retreat preached to the Sisters, Quasimodo Sunday 1989, 10th conf.

28 Conference given to the Sisters, September 19, 1974.

29 HOMEC 13A, September 18, 1977.

30 Retreat preached to the Sisters, September 1984, 11th conf.

31 Homily on the occasion of his priestly jubilee, September 23, 1979.

# AUGUST

1 *La sainteté sacerdotale*, 251-252.

2 Retreat preached to the Sisters, Quasimodo Sunday 1986, 9th conf.

3 *Ibid.*

4 CONFEC 29A, February 26, 1976.

5 Retreat preached to the Sisters, Quasimodo Sunday 1986, 9th conf.

6 *Le mystère de Jésus*, 64.

7 *La sainteté sacerdotale*, 252.

8 *Ibid.*, 251.

9 *Ibid.*

10 *La sainteté sacerdotale*, 253.

11 Homily for the Sisters, March 30, 1975.

12 Retreat preached to the Sisters, Quasimodo Sunday 1989, 9th conf.

13 Conference given in Mortain.

14 *La sainteté sacerdotale*, 255.

15 HOMEC 6A, November 29, 1975.

16 *La sainteté sacerdotale*, 255.

17 Homily for the Sisters, February 9, 1986.
18 Homily, Rouen, May 1, 1990 – Retreat preached to the Sisters, September 1984, 1st conf.
19 Homily, Lausanne, July 9, 1978.
20 Retreat preached to the Sisters, Quasimodo Sunday 1989, 1st conf.
21 Retreat preached to the Sisters, September 1984, 10th conf.
22 HOMEC 8B, August 22, 1976.
23 *La sainteté sacerdotale*, 253.
24 *Ibid.*, 256.
25 *Ibid.*, 255.
26 Retreat preached to the Sisters, Quasimodo Sunday 1989, 1st conf.
27 Retreat preached to the Sisters, Quasimodo Sunday 1986, 9th conf.
28 Retreat preached to the Sisters, September 1984, 10th conf.
29 Retreat preached to the Sisters, Quasimodo Sunday 1986, 9th conf.
30 *Ibid.*, 4th conf.
31 *Le mystère de Jésus*, 38-39.

# SEPTEMBER

1 HOMEC, April 17, 1977.
2 Homily for the Sisters, September 29, 1978.
3 Homily, Martigny, December 9, 1984.
4 Homily for the Sisters, July 25, 1976.
5 Retreat preached to the Sisters, September 1984, 9th conf.
6 Retreat preached to the Sisters, September 1976, 5th conf.
7 CONFEC 29a, February 26, 1976.
8 Retreat preached to the Sisters, September 1976, 9th conf.
9 Letter to Members, no. 4, November 18, 1978.
10 HOMEC 33B, June 29, 1985.
11 Retreat preached to the Sisters, September 1976, 2nd conf.
12 *Ibid.*
13 *Ibid.*
14 Retreat preached to the Sisters, September 1976, 1st conf.
15 *Ibid.*, 9th conf.

16 *Ibid.*

17 *Ibid.*

18 *Ibid.*

19 *Ibid.*

20 *Ibid.*

21 *Ibid.*

22 *Ibid.*

23 *Ibid.*

24 HOMEC 17A, February 11, 1979.

25 Retreat preached to the Sisters, September 1976, 8th conf.

26 *Le mystère de Jésus*, 111.

27 Retreat preached to the Sisters, September 1976, 5th conf.

28 Homily for the Sisters, Quasimodo Sunday 1977.

29 *Itinéraire spirituel*, 17.

30 Conference given to the Sisters, July 24, 1975.

# OCTOBER

1 *Ils l'ont décoronné* [*They Have Uncrowned Him*] (Clovis), 246.

2 Homily, Besançon, September 5, 1976.

3 HOMEC 8B, August 22, 1976.

4 Retreat preached to the Sisters, Quasimodo Sunday 1989, 6th conf.

5 Conference, Angers, November 23, 1980.

6 Retreat preached to the Sisters, Quasimodo Sunday 1989, 5th conf.

7 Homily for the Sisters, July 25, 1976.

8 Homily, Lille, August 29, 1976.

9 HOMEC, August 22, 1976.

10 Retreat preached to the Sisters, Quasimodo Sunday 1989, 5th conf.

11 Homily for the Sisters, July 25, 1976.

12 *Ibid.*

13 *Ils l'ont décoronné*, 251.

14 Retreat preached to the Sisters, Quasimodo Sunday 1989, 6th conf.

15 Letter to Members, no. 3, Christmas 1977.

16 HOMEC 14B, June 29, 1978.

17 Retreat preached to the Sisters, Quasimodo Sunday 1989, 5th conf.
18 Homily, Lille, August 29, 1976.
19 *Itinéraire spirituel*, 29-30.
20 Retreat preached to the Sisters, Quasimodo Sunday 1988, 1st and only conf.
21 *Ils l'ont découronné*, 251.
22 Retreat preached to the Sisters, Quasimodo Sunday 1989, 5th conf.
23 *Ibid.*
24 *Ils l'ont découronné*, 245.
25 *Ibid.*, 245-246.
26 *Ibid.*, Introduction.
27 Homily, Besançon, September 5, 1976.
28 Letter to Members, no. 3, Christmas 1977.
29 Homily on the occasion of his Priestly Jubilee, September 23, 1979.
30 Homily for the Sisters, April 18, 1976.
31 *Itinéraire spirituel*, 30.

# NOVEMBER

1 HOMEC 46B, November 1, 1990.
2 *Itinéraire spirituel*, 80.
3 HOMEC 27A, March 4, 1983.
4 HOMEC 16A, November 1, 1978.
5 *Itinéraire spirituel*, 80.
6 HOMEC 16A, November 1, 1978.
7 *Ibid.*
8 *Ibid.*
9 Homily, Saint John Lateran, May 24, 1975 – *Itinéraire spirituel*, 91-93.
10 HOMEC 13B, November 1, 1977.
11 CONFEC 16A, January 27, 1975.
12 HOMEC 17B, April 17, 1979.
13 *Le mystère de Jésus*, 121-122.
14 Easter retreat, Écône, 1975, 4th conf.
15 HOMEC 6A, November 29, 1979.

16 Easter retreat, Écône, 1975, 4th conf.
17 HOMEC 2A, February 3, 1974.
18 HOMEC 17B, Easter 1979.
19 *Le mystère de Jésus*, 39.
20 HOMEC 40B, October 3, 1987.
21 HOMEC 46A, Easter 1990.
22 HOMEC 9A, January 1, 1976.
23 HOMEC 15A, Easter 1978.
24 Homily for the Sisters, June 2, 1989.
25 Easter retreat, Écône, 1975, 3rd conf.
26 HOMEC 47A, August 15, 1990.
27 Homily, August 15, 1976 or 1977.
28 HOMEC 16A, Christmas 1978.
29 HOMEC 6A, November 29, 1975.
30 Homily for the Sisters, Quasimodo Sunday 1977.

# DECEMBER

1  HOMEC 16A and 29A, Christmas 1978 and 1983.
2  HOMEC 29A, Christmas 1983.
3  HOMEC 6A and 29A, Christmas 1975 and 1983.
4  *Le mystère de Jésus*, 96.
5  *Ibid.*, 100 and 103.
6  *Ibid.*, 123.
7  *Ibid.*, 127.
8  HOMEC 1B, December 8, 1972.
9  HOMEC 6A, Christmas 1975.
10 CONFEC 8A, June 5, 1974.
11 *Itinéraire spirituel*, 50.
12 *Ibid.*
13 *Le mystère de Jésus*, 97.
14 Easter Retreat, Écône, 1975, 3rd conf.
15 CONFEC 8B, June 6, 1974 (*Fideliter* no. 95).
16 *Itinéraire spirituel*, 58.
17 Retreat preached to the Sisters, Quasimodo Sunday 1986, 9th
      conf.
18 *La messe de toujours*, 74.
19 HOMEC 6A, Christmas 1975.

20 *Itinéraire spirituel*, 72.
21 *Le mystère de Jésus*, 114.
22 HOMEC 29A, Christmas 1983.
23 HOMEC 24A, February 2, 1982.
24 HOMEC 6A, Christmas 1975.
25 HOMEC 29A, Christmas 1983.
26 HOMEC 6B, April 3, 1976.
27 Homily, Saint John Lateran, May 24, 1975.
28 HOMEC 6A, Christmas 1975.
29 HOMEC 19B, Christmas 1979.
30 *Ibid.*
31 HOMEC 6A, Christmas 1975.

# Archbishop
# Marcel Lefebvre

## Chronological Overview

**1905:** *November 29*: born in Tourcoing. *November 30*: baptized at Tourcoing.

**1910:** *December 25*: First Holy Communion, writes to St. Pius X.

**1923:** *October 25*: enters the French Seminary in Rome then under the direction of Fr. Le Floch.

**1926-27:** Condemnation of Action Française. Military service at Valenciennes.

**1929:** *September 21*: ordained priest in Lille by Cardinal Liénart.

**1930-31:** Curate at Lomme, working class area of Lille.

**1931:** *September 1*: enters novitiate of the Holy Ghost Fathers at Orly.

**1932:** *September 8*: religious profession. *November 12*: sails from Bordeaux for Gabon as a missionary.

**1935:** *September 25*: perpetual vows in religion.

**1945:** *October 16*: appointed superior of the scholasticate at Mortain in Normandy.

**1947:** *June 12*: appointed Vicar Apostolic of Dakar. *September 18*: consecrated bishop at Tourcoing by Cardinal Liénart.

**1948:** *September 22*: appointed Apostolic Delegate for French Black Africa and Madagascar, with the rank of archbishop.

**1955:** *September 14*: made first Archbishop of Dakar.

**1958:** *June 12*: receives the pallium.

**1959:** *July 22*: relieved of duties as Apostolic Delegate but remains Archbishop of Dakar.

**1960:** *November 15*: appointed Assistant to the Pontifical Throne.

**1962:** *January 23*: reassigned to diocese of Tulle with the title of Archbishop-Bishop. *March 13*: appointed consulter to the Sacred Congregation de Propaganda Fide. *July 26*: elected (recommended) Superior General of the Holy Ghost Fathers.

**1962-65:** Council Father and resistance leader during the Second Vatican Council.

**1968:** *October 28*: leaves his post of Superior General during the General Chapter for the "renovation" of his congregation.

**1969:** *October 13*: opens "International House of St. Pius X" in Fribourg with encouragement of local bishop.

**1970:** *October 1*: with permission from bishop of Sion, opens a "year of spirituality" at Ecône in Valais, Switzerland, as a prelude to seminary studies. *November 1*: receives from Bishop Charrière of Fribourg official approval for the Priestly Society of Saint Pius X for six years *ad experimentum*.

**1974:** *November 11-13*: Apostolic visit of seminary at Ecône. *November 21*: Archbishop Lefebvre's "declaration."

**1975:** *May 6*: Approval for the Priestly Society of Saint Pius X is withdrawn by His Excellency Bishop Pierre Mamie, successor of Bishop Charrière.

**1976:** *July 1*: *suspens a divinis* by Pope Paul VI. *August 29*: celebrates the "forbidden Mass" at Lille, which makes his fight known to the world.

**1978:** *August 6*: death of Paul VI. *September 29*: death of John Paul I. *October 16*: election of John Paul II. *November 18*: audience with John Paul II.

**1983:** *November 21*: with Bishop de Castro Mayer sends open letter to the Pope.

**1986:** *August 27, September 28, December 2*: protests against the "scandal" of the interreligious meeting chaired by John Paul II at Assisi.

**1988:** *June 30*: consecrates four bishops at Ecône with the pontifical mandate "of the Church of all time."

**1991:** *March 25*: death in Martigny, Valais, Switzerland.